TEDDY BEARS

TEDDY BEARS

THE COLLECTOR'S GUIDE TO SELECTING, RESTORING, AND ENJOYING NEW AND VINTAGE TEDDY BEARS

Margaret and Gerry Grey

COURAGE BOOKS

Canadian Representatives:
General Publishing Co., Ltd.
30 Lesmill Road, Don Mills
Ontario M3B 2T6

9 8 7 6 5 4 3 2 1
Digit on the right indicates the number of this printing

Library of Congress
Cataloging-in-Publication Number
93-074691

ISBN 1-56138-434-8

This book was designed and produced by
Quintet Publishing Limited
6 Blundell Street
London N7 9BH

Creative Director: Richard Dewing
Designer: Ian Hunt
Project Editor: Katie Preston
Editor: Alison Leach
Photographers: Nick Bailey and Jeremy Thomas

Typeset in Great Britain by
Central Southern Typesetters, Eastbourne
Manufactured in Singapore by
Bright Arts Pte Limited
Printed in China by
Leefung-Asco Printers Limited

AUTHORS' DEDICATION
To mum, dad and family and all of our teddy bear
friends the world over. Particular thanks and
appreciation to those people past, present and future
who ever wanted to write about or make a teddy bear
– without their pioneering spirit there would be no
need for this book. And especially to grandson Karl,
who seems to have inherited our love and enthusiasm
for teddy bears.

Published by Courage Books
an imprint of Running Press Book Publishers
125 South Twenty-second Street
Philadelphia, Pennsylvania 19103-4399

CONTENTS

INTRODUCTION 6

1 FROM TOY BEAR TO TEDDY BEAR (1903–18) 9

2 BETWEEN THE WARS (1919–39) 19

3 POST-WAR RECOVERY (1946–60) 30

4 THE AGE OF SPECIAL EDITION BEARS 40

5 THE ERA OF THE TEDDY BEAR ARTIST 54

6 WHERE AND HOW TO BUY 66

7 CARE AND REPAIRS 73

8 LEARNING MORE ABOUT BEARS 77

INDEX 79

ACKNOWLEDGMENTS 80

INTRODUCTION

It is only about 15 years since a talented but obscure actor, Peter Bull, whose face was instantly recognizable but whose name is hardly ever remembered, first alerted people to the joys of collecting teddy bears by talking with such enthusiasm about them on British and American television. At the time it was unusual to know precisely what an arctophile is — a person who loves teddy bears — let alone be a collector of teddy bears.

The U.S., which was and still is the world's leading teddy-bear nation, provided the necessary driving force for this new phenomenon to continue into the 1980s, but several years passed before it spread to other parts of the world. Teddy bear collecting is now, however, one of the most popular collecting interests worldwide. Prices for all bears have escalated in recent years, culminating in the record-breaking sale at auction (for $86,000) of "Happy" in 1989. All collectors naturally live in hope that one day they will find their own "Happy," but teddy-bear collecting is much more than good investment.

Over the years, many authors have tried to analyze precisely what the appeal of a teddy bear is. Although

LEFT **The bear on the left is a Gebrüder Bing from 1911; on the right is a Chiltern Hugmee c. 1930.**

ABOVE **"Happy" – a 1926 Steiff – is seen here in her role as mascot of the authors' "Teddies of the World '93" convention.**

this is challenging, we think it is quite unnecessary and probably an impossible task. In our opinion though, "Happy" seems to epitomize the sheer beauty and character we all seek in our teddy bears – gaze into those great big eyes and your heart just melts! It is precisely this reaction that should be experienced with any bear – love and appreciation – rather than thinking about its potential as an investment. Collect only what appeals to you and not just what you think might be valuable; that way, you will not be disappointed. In fact, for the majority of people, the most "precious" bear, regardless of financial investment, in their collection will be the first bear they ever owned, loved, and cherished since childhood.

RIGHT **A highly collectible cinnamon center seam Steiff from 1905, measuring 16 inches.**

LEFT **An early (1930s) art silk plush blue bear by Chad Valley (15½ inches). Note the red foot label and the large nose, both typical of the era.**

BELOW **A Steiff Zotty measuring 11 inches. Zotty was a new style first produced in the 1950s, and this cinnamon mohair bear is a fine example of the appeal these have for collectors.**

BELOW **This lovely bear from J. K. Farnell was made in the early 1920s and measures 18 inches. It is made from** mohair and filled with excelsior. Note Farnell's distinctive five-webbed claw pattern.

BELOW **"Edelweiss" made by Steiff in 1909 and measuring 16 inches. Note the metal button in the left ear inscribed "STEIFF" with *"FF"* underscored.**

This book is intended to provide you with examples of some of the bears you might wish to add to your collection and tell you more about those you already have. It is not about what we own or want to collect – although some of our preferences are naturally given – but more a cross section of collectible bears to help guide you. In a book of this size, it is impossible to do justice to the whole spectrum of bears, and we have concentrated in general on bears that are available and therefore affordable, although a few rare examples have been included. So, whether your preference is for "old" bears (pre-1960), contemporary manufactured bears, or artist-designed teddy bears, good bear-hunting and good luck!

LEFT **A one-off artist bear by Barbara Conley c. 1993, measuring 22 inches. Using traditional materials, Barbara manages to recapture the character of the early bears.**

RIGHT **These one-off bears were produced for the authors in 1991. They are the result of a collaboration between two of the world's top artists – Joan Woessner and Steve Schutt.**

THE ORIGINAL TEDDY BEAR MAN

In the late 1970s, Peter Bull (PB) brought about a great change in the teddy-bear world. Because he readily talked about his passion for bears, people felt they, too, could openly admit to caring for and amassing hordes of old and new teddy bears. Contrary to popular belief, PB was not a collector, but his doors were ever open to "waifs and strays." His favorites were probably "Theodore," "Delicatessen," and "Bully" bear. Following Theodore's appearance on *The Tonight Show*, a Miss Euphemia Ladd of Sacco, Maine, asked if her old bear could come and live with "Theodore." The bear was christened "Delicatessen" and was later to star as "Aloysius" in the television series *Brideshead Revisited*. On May 21, 1984, Peter Bull, DSC, died of a heart attack aged 72. He is sadly missed, but he would be delighted if he could see the fun and joy that resulted from his efforts.

FROM TOY BEAR TO TEDDY BEAR (1903–18)

CHAPTER

The true origins of the teddy bear probably go back to the Middle Ages when so-called civilized people were fascinated by real wild bears. Unfortunately, these poor tortured and abused beasts were used throughout Europe purely for entertainment – as dancing bears. Hundreds of years later, the Victorians began the trend for real bears to be kept in zoos – again for the entertainment and education of the masses.

At the end of the 19th century, Stuttgart Zoo in Germany was frequently visited by a young toy designer from Giengen-en-Brenz named Richard Steiff, a nephew of the renowned toy producer Margarete Steiff. He was interested in all animals, but bears particularly intrigued him. Lifelike bears had been made by Steiff for some five or six years previously, but they were based on fully grown bears and were therefore difficult to play with. Richard sketched little bear cubs, and it was these that influenced Steiff's prototype of the first toy bear late in 1902.

This toy bear was part of a small range of movable (*Beweglich*) animals employing disk joints (*angeschiebt*), which formed part of a shipment of toys to New York in the middle of February, 1903. Its general shape and appearance closely resembled a real bear with a long shaven snout, very long arms, stout body, big feet, and the quite distinctive back hump.

It is important to consider the period of time required for designing and then producing this new range. Clifford Berryman's famous cartoon of President Theodore (Teddy) Roosevelt appeared in the *Washington Post* on November 16, 1902. Communications in those days were so limited that we doubt that this cartoon could have had any influence on Richard Steiff, as is often suggested.

However, it is thought, though not substantiated, that the cartoon was the impetus for Russian immigrants Morris and Rose Michtom, who were novelty and stationery storekeepers in Brooklyn, New York, to create the first toy bears made in America.

LEFT **The 1908 cover of *The Sketch* picturing a teddy bear at the Chicago rally to elect President Taft. The caption is "Teddy Bear in Politics: the Cause of the Rumpus."**

Subsequently – and presumably rather later in 1903 – the Michtoms' toy bears were bought by a large wholesale company, Butler Bros., and distributed throughout the U.S.

We believe it would take a considerable time to design, develop, and then make a line of quality prototype toys for export. Common sense therefore suggests that Steiff's own toy bear was in fact the world's first! However, both Steiff and the Michtoms, who set up The Ideal Novelty and Toy Co., can justly claim they were pioneers of the original teddy bear. The dramatic last-minute purchase of 3,000 of Steiff's bears at the Leipzig Toy Fair in March 1903 by Herman Berg of Geo Borgfeldt, world-famous American toy importers, when everyone else had ignored them, was incredibly fortuitous.

While Steiff's bear closely resembles a real bear, the Ideal version is much more similar to Berryman's own cartoon bear cub and, therefore, rather more like the teddy bear we know. Clifford Berryman continued to draw many cartoons associated with President Roosevelt, and eventually, they were probably the greatest single influence in coining the term "teddy bear" that we now so affectionately use.

During those early years, both firms developed their lines, but it was not very long before Steiff's greater experience of toy design and production, coupled with Richard's imaginative ideas for bears of such variety and sheer quality, enabled them to become the world's premier manufacturer. Conversely, Ideal's bears appear to have hardly changed from their first design.

Steiff's first bear in 1903 was referred to as the 55PB, followed by the 35PB in early 1904. Both used disk joints held together by a strong string cord. Unfortunately, this cord was found to be rather impractical, and it broke so easily that Steiff changed briefly to using double wires, but this proved to be far too dangerous. This led quickly to the development of the famous rod bears where a metal rod was passed through the upper body of the bear attaching the arms, with a vertical T-rod connecting and supporting the head, and another rod attaching the legs. The head was stuffed from the top and to facilitate this, a horizontal seam from ear to ear was provided. This bear is usually referred to as the 28PB.

Unfortunately, this bear was rather awkward in its movement, and its large rotund body really did not have enough "child appeal." After only a year (1905), production began on the *Barle* (meaning someone dear) range of PAB bears. Their great virtue was that they were softer, filled with a mixture of excelsior and kapok, making them far more cuddly than their

LEFT **"Charlamagne" by Ideal,** *c.* **1903/4 and measuring 20 inches. Ideal was only able to sustain this quality and style for about five years.**

RIGHT **"Christian Gabriel" by Steiff** *c.* **1903/4, measuring 15 inches. These rod bears are among the most desirable of early Steiffs, especially with the original wax nose.**

predecessors, and significantly more appealing to children!

This was a great breakthrough and the turning point for Steiff, which had experienced great difficulty during the first few years with acceptance of its toy bears. The PAB35 is assumed to have been the first of a line that came in seven sizes from 6½ to 32 inches, but because the bear was lighter in weight and the jointed body was held together by a conventional double disk joint and metal pin, it had a more acceptable and reliable movement. (Incidentally, to establish the size of this line of bears, always measure in the *seated* position to the top of its head.)

Around the same time, Richard Steiff also produced his now famous prototype – a small gray bear referred to as model 5322 (5 = movable, 3 = mohair, and 22 = size (13 inches). Steiff's archives suggest that only two of these were made and perhaps a few others as samples. Quite definitely, it must be one of the rarest and possibly the most valuable bear on earth. An example can be found in the Steiff Museum.

Franz Steiff, another of Margarete's nephews, had the previous year decided to implement a trademark standard by introducing the metal button in the ear "Knopf im Ohr," a symbol used ever since. Initially, the elephant button was used, followed later that year

LEFT **The nickel-plated Steiff elephant button is supposed to have been the first unregistered trademark "Knopf im Ohr." It was followed by a blank button and then in 1905 by a button embossed with "STEIFF."**

(1904) by a plain blank button (not to be confused with the blank blue button used briefly between 1948 and 1950), superseded in May 1905 by an inscribed STEIFF button when Steiff finally had its unique trademark confirmed.

There is some controversy over the exact dating of the buttons – most authorities now suggest the order we give, but others believe the blank button came first. Both may have been used simultaneously, although we suspect the elephant button was possibly the first because it happened to be Steiff's logo at the time. Logic, however, suggests the blank button might have been used initially simply because it was easier and more convenient to produce. In the U.S. in 1906, the name "Teddy" was adopted, and the ubiquitous "teddy bear" was officially christened.

Meanwhile, in the U.S. teddy-bear manufacturers were emerging (mainly around New York), who

LEFT **This PAB 43 (right) from 1905 is shown here with a modern replica of a PAB 35. The original bear marked a successful change of direction for Steiff.**

RIGHT **"Still Hope" by Aetna from c. 1907/08. This company was probably the best American bear maker in the early days, as can be seen from this lovely example.**

probably drew on the experience and knowledge of immigrant toy workers flocking in from Europe. Despite innumerable claims by American manufacturers that their bears compared in quality to those from Steiff, they emphatically did not! One thing, however, we can thank the early American firms for was their inventiveness – bears that whistled, musical bears, and of course the redoubtable bright-eyed teddy, which had eyes illuminated by an inbuilt battery – were but a few of the intriguing new features they gave to teddy bears. It was this flair for the unusual that influenced manufacturers in other countries, including Germany.

Teddy bear manufacture did not begin in Britain until 1908 when J. K. Farnell began production. Unfortunately, the British public was not immediately enthralled by its bears, and Farnells was forced to export almost its entire stock to the U.S., South Africa, and even Germany! Evidence of other British manufacturers from this period is very sketchy and unreliable, and positive identification will be difficult.

The world trade in teddy bears reached its peak in 1907 when Steiff's production alone was a little under 1,000,000 teddy bears. Some companies that sprang up simply produced imitations of Steiff bears, but there were innovators such as Gebrüder Bing, which was responsible for developing the wind-up mechanism for bears (1908–10) used for roller-skating bears, acrobatic or tumbling bears, and even bears pushing balls. The boom was followed almost immediately by a slump, during which several manufacturers in Germany and the U.S. ceased trading overnight. Some new companies did appear such as Schuco (Schreyer and Co) and Gebrüder Hermann Kg. With the outbreak of war in 1914, German goods were prohibited in Britain, and the instant demise of the competition persuaded several British companies to start teddy-bear production. Many companies began by copying Steiff products, but it was not long before skills developed enough to start producing original designs for good-quality bears.

LEFT **"Sergeant Culver"**, *c.* 1907/08, measures 20¼ inches. The manufacturer of this splendid bear is unknown.

BELOW **A splendid cinnamon Steiff measuring 15¾ inches. It** was made at the height of Steiff's early success *c.* 1907/08.

RIGHT **This bright-eyes bear was made by the Stuffed Toy Co.** *c.* 1917 and measures 17 inches.

COLLECTOR'S NOTEBOOK 1903–18

These early formative years provide the serious collector with their greatest challenge and, needless to say, expense. Fortunately, many top-quality teddy bears have survived, and what wonderful and lovable characters they can be. (Note: the dates indicate the first known year of production.)

U.S.A.

AETNA TOY ANIMAL CO. (1906)

❚ Look for the printed oval trademark "AETNA," usually stamped across the center of the bear's left foot pad; quite often indistinct, but traces can usually be found if you look carefully.

❚ These bears are wonderful, with such lovely, appealing faces, and, in our view, probably represent the best of all American bears from this period.

❚ Rare and extremely hard to find because the firm only existed for about two years; very collectible.

BELOW **A bear from the Bruin Manufacturing Co. c. 1907/08, measuring 12½ inches. Many American companies failed after only a few years, and this makes their bears even more desirable and sought after.**

BRUIN MANUFACTURING CO. (1907)

❚ Look for the woven black label with B.M.C. inscribed in gold letters and fixed centrally across the breadth of the right foot.

❚ The bears have wide-set ears with rather triangular shaped heads.

❚ These bears are highly collectible though scarce because this firm only existed from about 1907 to 1909.

HARMAN MANUFACTURING CO. (1907)

❚ Appearance rather similar to Ideal bears which could create identification difficulties. Something unusual to look for is a "Teddy Shopper" (handbag size) in white or cinnamon mohair which came in three sizes (10, 12, and 14 inches).

HECLA BEAR CO. (1907)

❚ These attractive bears will be particularly difficult to identify due to their close resemblance to Steiff bears of the same period. They appear, however, to stand rather differently, and the wide placing of the ears appears more typical of American bears than Steiff.

❚ Rust-colored yarn was normally used for forming noses and mouths.

IDEAL TOY AND NOVELTY CO. (1903)

The first of the American bear manufacturers. Early examples are very elusive and difficult to authenticate. The appearance of Ideal bears is, however, quite distinctive, and they are very appealing and collectible.

❚ Unfortunately, the company seems to have adopted similar designs for quite a long time, and to some extent this detracts from their collectibility.

❚ It should be possible to find bears from this era in good condition and not too expensive when compared with German bears of the same genre.

❚ Look particularly for the small 6-inch googly-eyed bear made about 1904 and based on the Clifford Berryman cartoon (supposed to have been given away during Theodore Roosevelt's election campaign). A larger 12-inch size continued to be made until *circa* 1912 and is not so valuable.

RIGHT **This bear c. 1908, measuring 15¾ inches, marks the end of an era for Ideal – America's first bear manufacturer. In later years, quality changed radically.**

OTHER AMERICAN MANUFACTURERS

THE AMERICAN DOLL & TOY MANUFACTURING CO. (1907) Produced electric bright-eyed teddies and the celebrated "White House" teddy bear with a voice, ribbon, and bell, rather similar to Steiff except for flat-bottomed feet. Claimed their bears were the only American-made bears to be equal to the imported bears (Steiff). Sole agents were Baker and Gigler Company.

COLUMBIA TEDDY BEAR MANUFACTURING (1907) Were responsible for the "Laughing Roosevelt" bears which can still be found, albeit with difficulty.

DREAMLAND DOLL COMPANY (1907) Produced a topsy-turvy half teddy–half doll separated by skirt. Rare and hard to find.

B. EPSTEIN (1907) Little known except they advertised their bears in 1907 (*Playthings*).

FAST BLACK SHIRT CO. (1907) Produced teddy bears with electric bright eyes.

MRS. G.C. GILLISPIE (1907) Produced and patented a tumbling teddy bear.

GUND MANUFACTURING CO. (1906) Thought to have produced a small line of teddy bears, but these early bears have so far not been definitely identified.

ABOVE **A "Laughing Roosevelt" bear from Columbia Teddy Bear Manufacturers c. 1907 measuring 17 inches. The mouth can be operated by squeezing the stomach.**

HAHN AND AMBERG (1907) Advertised their teddy-bear dolls.

MILLAR MANUFACTURING CO. (1906) Advertised in 1907 the "'Antiseptic Bear' for the most cleanliness" which came in cinnamon, white, and other unspecified colors.

ROUECH-BOWDEN (1907) A company from Chicago and another which appears to have based its designs on Steiff.

STRAUSS MANUFACTURING CO. (1907) Produced wonderful musical and self-whistling teddy bears.

UNCLE REMUS STUFFED TOYS (1907) Distributed by A.S. Ferguson & Company, Uncle Remus produced bears with a special patented eye-fixing method which meant "permanent uniformity" in positioning the eyes and retaining the head shape. Could have been based on Charles Sackmans' invention patent 844,619 November, 1908.

WHITESON COMPANY (1907) Advertised "Prices The Lowest: Largest Sizes and Workmanship the Best," but nothing else is known.

TEDDY DISTRIBUTORS IN THE U.S.A.

Influential importers/wholesalers who distributed teddy bears throughout the U.S. at the time are worth mentioning. Many of them persuaded manufacturers to make and supply bears, some of which they may have marketed under their own names.

GEO. BORGFELDT & COMPANY was the greatest of all these firms and was responsible for that first eventful purchase of 3,000 teddy bears from Steiff at the Leipzig Spring Toy Fair in 1903. Had they not done this, we might never have had a teddy-bear craze at all! Borgfeldt's influence on the toy industry was legendary.

BUTLER BROS. subsequently took over the marketing and distribution of the early Ideal Toy and Novelty Co. teddy bears. It also distributed a line of Steiff bears from about 1908.

STROBEL & WILKEN CO. was notable as distributor for BMC.

E.L. HORSMAN & COMPANY was distributor for Hecla and Aetna bears (*see* page 13). It was Horsman & Co. who first used the name "teddy" in an advertisement in the American trade magazine *Playthings* in December, 1906.

BRITAIN

ATLAS MANUFACTURING CO. (1914)

This was another firm who changed from making sporting goods to teddy bears.

▮ In 1916 *The Toy and Fancy Goods Trader* reported the Atlas line as 30 varieties of teddies from 8½ inches to 7 feet high; colored gold, white or light brown, and with squeakers, chimes, and rattles.

▮ As with so many of the early British firms, very little evidence exists to support identification, but as far as we can tell, the bodies of the bears were more like German ones in style, but the hands were large and round, with small flattish faces, wide-set ears and noses which might possibly have had down-turned outer stitching, and inverted Y-shaped mouths stitched tight under their noses.

BASSETT LOWKE (1910)

This firm was best known for its production of tin-plate toys, particularly railroads, but it was reported as having also produced teddy bears.

▮ The great German firm, Gebrüder Bing, which also made locomotives for Bassett Lowke, introduced bears to its line, so it seems probable BL should have done likewise, and it is also conceivable they might have been Bing bears as well. Unfortunately, no records or examples of these bears have so far been found, so we shall probably never be sure.

CHAD VALLEY CO. LTD. (1914)

Chad Valley was one of Britain's most successful toy manufacturers.

▮ A retrospective editorial published in *The Toy and Fancy Goods Trader* in August, 1922, reported that Chad Valley actually began production of its first teddy bear early in 1914 before the outbreak of war.

▮ Frustratingly, no other supportive evidence exists as to the appearance of the bear, but we suspect it would probably be similar to the bears the company produced in the early 1920s, but of course without the early "Chad Valley" or "Aerolite" button, which was not registered until 1923.

DEANS RAG BOOK CO. LTD. (1915)

One of Britain's longest established toymakers.

▮ Although it had made its famous cutout cloth patterns of teddy bears as early as 1908, apparently it was not until 1915 that Deans decided to make its first teddy bear.

▮ No positive details of these bears are currently known.

J.K. FARNELL (1908)

There is simply not enough evidence to identify the first bears produced by Farnell positively.

▮ Despite Farnell's excellent reputation, teddies were not at all popular with the home market, and the company exported most of its production. These early examples are now more likely to be found in the U.S. than in Britain.

▮ For the moment at least, we can only speculate, but a definite pre-1920 Farnell is unknown.

▮ We suspect these teddy bears will probably be somewhat similar to the better-known Alpha line of bears produced from the beginning of the 1920s, although as yet we cannot prove this.

HARWIN & COMPANY (1915)

These bears were very close to Steiff products – not surprising really because the sales manager, Mr. F. Taylor, represented Steiff for some years!

▮ Harwins is best known for its line of "Ally" bears produced in 1916 – these were bears dressed in various uniforms: British, Scottish, Russian; soldiers, sailors, and nurses.

▮ Boy and girl teddies were also produced, and in 1917 a teddy bear in pajamas appeared.

▮ These bears will be quite difficult to find, particularly in good condition and with their original clothes, and will be among the more expensive British bears from this period.

LEON REES & CO. (1915)

In 1915 at its Chiltern Toy Works, L. Rees & Co. produced the original Chiltern bear – "Master Teddy."

▮ This rather curious rotund fat-headed little teddy had googly eyes, was dressed in pink and white striped shirt with large bib-type collar, ribbon bow tie, and very

BELOW **This is the earliest "Master Teddy," and as the first Chiltern bear (*c.* 1915), it is rare. It measures 10 inches.**

high-waisted blue pants with a patch. It has a little red tongue.

▌ It appears to have been available in five sizes, and although rare they do exist; good-quality ones are expensive.

▌ The first advertisements (1915) indicate the patch was on the left leg and without a chest tag, but we have seen bears with the patch on the right leg and with a chest tag indicating "US patent applied for"; these would have been made a year or two later.

W.J. TERRY (1913)

This firm used the trade name "Terryer Toys."

▌ Its early bears began to establish the stereotype British look, rather than just copying German makers as many others did.

▌ Examples from early advertisements suggest the bears had eyes which glared, large round heads, and rather big ears.

▌ Positive identification is difficult.

OTHER BRITISH MANUFACTURERS

THOMAS BAXTER (1915) Produced an illuminated electric eye teddy bear.

THE BRITISH UNITED TOY MANUFACTURING CO. (1914) Used the trademark "OMEGA" for their stuffed-toy line, including bears and "CAMWHEEL" for a stuffed toy attached to a metal frame with wooden wheels (similar to the Steiff Record line.)

CRAY AND NICHOLLS (1916) Reported to have made bears at this time, but no records exist.

EAST LONDON TOY FACTORY (1915) Used the trademark "EALON" for their line of stuffed toys. Examples of these early bears remain unidentified.

GOTTSCHALK AND DAVIS (1915) Manufactured bears characterized by ears set very high on top of head with a very stern-looking face and arms rather high on shoulders.

HAWKSLEY & CO. (LIVERPOOL) LTD. (1916) Usually produced bears on wheels, similar to Steiff in style and quality.

IMPERIAL TOY CO. (1916) Reported to have made bears at this time, but no records exist.

ISAACS (1915) Used the trade name "ISA" (eventually taken over by Chad Valley Co. Ltd.)

TEDDY DISTRIBUTORS IN BRITAIN

During these early formative years, there were two major importers and distributors in Britain.

Josef Eisenmann, or "Jo" as he was popularly known, was acknowledged as the "King of the Toy Trade" in the U.K. Eisenmann & Co. imported and distributed toys, particularly those from Germany, but it was Jo who suggested to J.K. Farnell that it should make teddy bears to combat the influx of Steiff products. Jo was also the father-in-law of Leon Rees, who eventually in 1920 collaborated with Harry G. Stone to take over the manufacturer of the famous "Chiltern" line.

From 1899 until the outbreak of World War I in 1914, **Herbert E. Hughes** was the sole importer of Steiff products to the U.K. In the Ciesliks' book, *Button in the Ear*, they report the close relationship that existed between Otto Steiff and Herbert. Hughes's major clients in Britain were Harrods, Hamleys, Gamages, and Josef Eisenmann himself. Because of this association, Herbert would almost certainly have had a detailed knowledge of Steiff and the German industry. In 1908 he was responsible for an order of *40,000* Steiff bears just for Britain. Hughes ceased his involvement with Steiff at the outbreak of World War I.

LEFT **"King Arthur" by Steiff c. 1905, measuring 28¾ inches. These silver-white mohair bears are highly sought.**

W.H. JONES (1916) Some of its bears appear to have had very round bodies and large heads with wide-set ears and large long arms with upturned wrists but shapeless rod-like legs slightly turned to "stump"-type feet. The noses were unusual, almost batwing-shaped with large turned-down outer stitches.

ROSS TOY WORKS (1916) Also used the trade name "HERCULES," so we presume it was associated with the Wholesale Toy Co.

SOUTH WALES TOY MANUFACTURING CO. (1917) Used the trade name "Madingland." Bears can be distinguished by their large ears set close together on top of the head, large nose, and long mouth having a rather glum expression. Well-proportioned bodies and arms with distinctive raised circular-shaped foot pads with very thick flat insole linings.

STEEVANS MUSICAL TOYS (1918) Produced musical chime bears, but little else is known at present.

TEDDY TOY COMPANY (1916) Eventually in the 1920s, it adopted the trade name "Softanlite" and claimed the bears would be beautiful and soft, always retaining their shape and their joints never becoming loose. Their early bears have not been identified.

WHOLESALE TOY COMPANY (1915) Used the brand name "Hercules," for their line of stuffed toys, which included teddy bears and a group of wheeled animals.

WORTHING TOY FACTORY (1915) Known to have produced teddy bears with the trademark "Humpty Dumpty Toys."

WREKIN TOY COMPANY (1916) Eventually taken over by Chad Valley Co. Ltd.

A. YOUNG & SON (1915) Used the trade-name "Jumbo Toys."

GERMANY

GEBRÜDER BING (1908)
This firm made highly desirable bears which are surprisingly far scarcer than those produced by Steiff at the time. Expect to have to pay high prices, especially for those still in good condition.

▌ The metal arrow-shaped tag attached in the bear's right ear dates from 1908 to about 1910.

RIGHT **This desirable Bing c. 1910, measuring 15¾ inches, still has its original silver button under its left arm.**

▌ A silver metal or orange button attached to the bear's left side under the arm inscribed with "GBN" suggests the period between 1910 and 1919.

▌ Any early Bing teddy bears, particularly those made from unusual colored mohair rather than the more conventional light to dark browns, will always be a great attribute to any collection.

ABOVE **This Bing bear c. 1911/12 measures 26¾ inches, and proves that long-nosed bears were made earlier than first thought.**

RIGHT **This Bing, measuring 13½ inches, from c. 1910 has an orange button attached to its left side.**

GEBRÜDER HERMANN (1911)

Records of these early bears do not appear to exist, and it would therefore be extremely difficult for anyone to identify positively bears from this era.

▌ The first labels ever used by Hermann were rosette-style, inscribed BEHA (*BE*rnard *HE*rmann) from about 1911 to 1929. An early Hermann would be a *real* find!

MARGARETE STEIFF (1903)

Without doubt the world's leading manufacturer, although its bears are highly desirable, they are likely to be extremely difficult to find and expensive. A typical example is the early rod bears from 1904.

▌ Should you ever find a 55PB, the first toy bear Steiff made, or a Richard Steiff gray teddy bear, then you could be looking at an absolute fortune.

▌ Any of the first PAB soft-filled bears will cost you a substantial amount of money.

▌ Black bears (only a small number were made around 1910–12), the hot-water bottle bear (only 90 were made between 1907 and 1914), or unusually colored bears are other valuable finds.

▌ Center-seam bears (1904–1906) have wonderful faces and are well regarded, but will also be expensive and scarce.

▌ Look for the rarer colors (white and cinnamon) and one with its original button in the left ear, but remember they will always attract a premium price.

OTHER GERMAN MANUFACTURERS

Bears made by any of the following firms will be very difficult to identify. There were many more manufacturers and thriving cottage-industries producing other stuffed toys, and it is almost certain some of them offered teddy bears in their line.

E. DEHLER (1910–11) No known details.

FLEISCHMANN & BLOEDEL (*circa* 1914) Used the trade name "MICHU."

CARL HARMUS, JR. (1909) Registered a design for a bear with a doll.

JOHANN HERMANN (1907) (SUCCEEDED BY **MAX HERMANN** (1920)) Examples of early bears are not known; throughout its time, the bears were very similar in appearance to those produced by cousins, Gebrüder Hermann. From 1920 on, the trademark "MAHESO" was adopted.

CARL HOFMANN & CO. (1910) Supposed to have produced the first black teddy bear.

ERICH LEISTNER (1910) Used the trade name "ERLE."

H. JOSEF LEVEN & SPRENGER (1910) No known details from this early period.

ERNST LIEBERMANN & CO. (1910) Used the trade name "ELI."

WILHELM STRUNZ (1908) Copied Steiff products, so therefore be careful. We would anticipate its bears to be of inferior quality and construction.

LEFT **These white Steiffs *c.* 1907/08, measuring 22 inches, are very collectible.**

BELOW **The Steiff PAB 43, *c.* 1905, 27½ inches, is a very rare soft-filled bear.**

BELOW **A popular center-seam Steiff *c.* 1905/06, measuring 15¾ inches.**

H.R.H. The DUCHESS of YORK.
A TEDDY FOR BABY ELIZABETH.

242.W.   BEAGLES
                         POSTCARDS.

BETWEEN THE WARS (1919–39)

CHAPTER 2

Immediately after World War I, a period of instability afflicted world markets, and many of the firms who had previously been producing teddy bears suddenly found themselves in financial trouble and had to cease trading.

Steiff, by then a well-established and world-leading manufacturer, experienced tremendous difficulty attempting to reestablish the preeminence it had enjoyed during the decade leading up to the war, and its struggle was intensified due mainly to a backlash of resentment in Britain and America. Broadly speaking, the German toy industry had no choice but to adopt lower prices during these inflationary times, and many organizations with a vested interest such as The British Toy Federation rather disparagingly referred to "cheap" German toys which the public should avoid!

The Japanese toy industry, in concert with many of the country's other industries at the time, were then beginning to expand, and their cheaper exports were becoming a threat to all. Elsewhere – France and Australia in particular – manufacturers began producing for their home markets.

The U.S. was the world's largest market for toys, but their own teddy-bear manufacturing base was by now much depleted. Unfortunately, very few of the new American companies of the time managed to make much of a name for themselves, with the possible exception of Knickerbocker, as consumers preferred the imported bears. Even well-established firms such as Ideal and Gund seemed to lack the ability to produce appealing teddy bears.

Britain, on the other hand, had rather successfully managed to retain almost all of its quality stuffed toy manufacturing base, and it was these companies who were subsequently able to prove their potential for producing original ideas. During the next two decades, several British companies were to establish themselves as equal to any. The most notable newcomer in the U.K. was Merrythought, established in 1930.

LEFT **A British postcard from c. 1936 showing the future Queen Elizabeth, the Queen Mother,** **holding a wonderful English bear from the era, probably by J. K. Farnell.**

ABOVE **This *c.* 1923 bear from J. K. Farnell (25 inches) has replacement pads, but the quality of early Alphas is apparent.**

ABOVE **This *c.* 1923/4 Chad Valley measures 17 inches and has the old cream-colored Aerolite trademark button in its ear.**

ABOVE **Despite its new nose, there is no mistaking this Schuco Yes-No mechanism bear *c.* 1930s, measuring 19 inches.**

ABOVE **A Peter bear by Gebrüder Süssenguth *c.* 1926, measuring 13¼ inches. The fierce appearance was not popular with children!**

ABOVE **This lovely white Steiff *c.* 1925/6 measures 13¾ inches. The remains of a red tag are still attached to the button.**

A popular feature of British bears at the time was the new style of soft-filled bears; the Teddy Toy Company produced "Softanlite," followed by W. J. Terry with "Ahsolight." Chad Valley had the "Aerolite" line, and many other manufacturers followed. There was also keen competition to present bears as hygienic toys, and the Institute of Hygiene mark of approval was highly coveted. In 1929, just before the Great Depression, the Teddy Toy Company introduced the new and cheaper art silk plush instead of mohair, while Chiltern followed shortly afterward with its "Silky" teddy and Farnell's "Silkalite" line.

In Germany, manufacturing had begun again after World War I, but Steiff was finding things difficult. For some years it had persisted with its old designs, until around 1925 when Richard Steiff wrote from the U.S. that Steiff bears "appear colorless, sober and insipid." These harsh words seemed just the jolt the company needed, and the result was a new generation of imaginative and original designs. It was at this time that "Happy" was produced, though it seems that very few bears of this type were made.

The firm Schreyer and Co., better known as Schuco, began this era with a unique bear design – the "Yes-No" series that had a mechanical linkage device concealed within the tail enabling the head to move up or down (nodding or shaking its head).

The Depression (1929–32) had severely weakened the foundations of virtually all teddy-bear manufacturers, and with the threat of another war, it is not surprising that the genre of bears made during the late 1930s lacked the variety of the previous 30 years.

COLLECTOR'S NOTEBOOK 1919–39

Due to the large number of teddy bear manufacturers all over the world at this time, you have a good chance of finding high-quality teddy bears from this era. However, many of the earlier bears, those from the 1920s for example, made by the more famous quality producers will be expensive.

U . S . A .

COMMONWEALTH TOY AND NOVELTY CO. (1934) 1937 saw the introduction of a rather unusual "Feed Me" bear.

▮ Teddy could be fed by pulling a cord at the back of his head so that his mouth would open to swallow food. The food could be retrieved by unzipping the bear. Although not very attractive, these bears are novel and certainly worth looking for.

GUND INC. (1906)

For a major company, it is quite surprising that there are so few examples of teddy bears they made during these early years. So far, few quality bears from this era have ever been properly identified, so these might be quite a find.

KNICKERBOCKER TOY CO. INC. (1920s)

This firm had been established for about 70 years when in the 1920s it began manufacturing teddy bears.

▮ Its bears are recognizable by their very wide heads and short snouts. Some of the early bears had metal noses, and others had conventional noses.

ABOVE **Despite the facial repairs, this is a good example of a Knickerbocker Toy Co. bear from the mid-1930s (17 inches).**

▮ Velveteen pads were used on these bears, and the firm seemed to like colored glass eyes, usually green.

▮ Knickerbocker bears had pale yellow cloth labels stitched into the chest seam with a horseshoe logo inscribed "Knickerbocker Toy Co. – New York."

▮ By far and away the best of the American bears made during this era, they remain relatively inexpensive.

B R I T A I N

CHAD VALLEY CO. LTD. (1914)

Under the banner of Chad Valley were a number of toy factories, but the teddy bears were made at the Wellington (Shropshire) factory.

ABOVE **A great character from Chad Valley from the early 1920s, measuring 28 inches. Its blue button is still attached to his throat.**

❚ Look for the lovely character bears with a very large triangular nose. However, a bear very reminiscent of this one was also advertised in 1935 so be very careful about dates.

❚ One way to tell the age is by the buttons Chad Valley used (if fitted). During the early 1920s, they had a broad steel rim with a flat recessed celluloid center; one "Chad Valley" button is colored blue, and the other "Aerolite" is colored cream. The "Chad Valley" button may be found attached to the bear's right ear, back, or throat. The "Aerolite" button is usually found on the bear's right ear.

❚ So far as we can tell, *circa* 1930 the buttons were changed for two new types – both the rim and celluloid center are flush, but the center is now raised and slightly convex. One button is cream colored and the other blue. These buttons are usually found in the right ear or sometimes on the left side.

❚ Magna (1930s) series of bears are really nice – look for the embroidered blue on white label on the sole of the right foot. Notice it refers to Harborne, which was Chad Valley's H.Q., although Chad Valley always stated it only ever made teddy bears at Wellington!

❚ Red lettering embroidered on a white label was introduced in the 1930s along with bears with large oval rather bulbous noses. These are great characters to add to your collection.

❚ Chad Valley constantly took over other toy companies either to improve the line or get rid of the competition. In the 1920s it took over Isaacs & Co., whose well-known trademark for stuffed toys (usually on wheels) had been ISA. In 1931, it acquired Peacock & Co. who had manufactured printed wooden blocks.

ABOVE **A Chad Valley c. 1930, measuring 16 inches, showing the distinctive bulbous nose and red label.**

ABOVE **An unusual Chad Valley "Pooh" bear c. 1929 measuring 8½ inches.**

ABOVE **The standing bear (25 inches) is from Chad Valley and has the later ear button. The other is by Peacock (27 inches). Both are from the mid-1930s.**

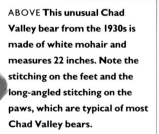

ABOVE **This unusual Chad Valley bear from the 1930s is made of white mohair and measures 22 inches. Note the stitching on the feet and the long-angled stitching on the paws, which are typical of most Chad Valley bears.**

Around the mid-1930s, Chad Valley introduced a "Peacock" bear which, so far as we can tell, was really a Chad Valley bear with a different label (red on white, style similar to Chad Valley except it carried the wording "Peacocks – British Toys – London."

An alternative, probably earlier label with a Peacock emblem is also known to exist. The Peacock bears we have seen are so remarkably similar to Chad Valley that we believe they were made in Chad's factory but marketed under the Peacock banner. They are rather scarce – a real find!

Any Chad Valley bears from this era are worth collecting, provided they are in good condition, and they ought not be too expensive.

In 1938 Chad Valley was awarded a "Royal Warrant," and a label on the sole of the left foot carries the Royal Coat of Arms and wording "Toymakers to Her Majesty the Queen." In 1953, this was changed (*see* page 32).

DEANS RAG BOOK CO. LTD. (1915)

It is surprisingly difficult to find Deans bears from this period, particularly in good condition.

Deans bears tend to have a triangular, flat-shaped head with wide-set, almost vertically located ears, which distinguishes them from other British bears.

Sadly, Deans bears may have been made from inferior quality mohair which might explain why they are nearly always found badly worn.

A straw-colored label with Deans Rag Book Co Ltd printed in black was stitched lengthwise along the sole of the foot. The reason these labels are often missing is because they were only attached at the ends.

ABOVE **Note the distinctive triangle-shaped head of this late 1930s Deans bear. It measures 17 inches.**

ABOVE **The odd proportions of this 1920s, Farnell suggest that the head and body came from different bears (23 inches).**

ABOVE **A Farnells bear *c.* 1925 showing typical webbed claws and cardboard inserts in canvas feet (19½ inches).**

J. K. FARNELL (1908)

Look for the early "Alpha" bears produced in the 1920s; the large bears are the best, always made using top-quality mohair, filled either with excelsior or kapok or a mixture of both.

Look particularly for the bears with very distinctive webbing on the paws. The Farnell webbing is quite different

ABOVE **One of the new style of Farnells bears *c.* 1935 that appeared after the factory fire in 1934 (16 inches).**

from that used by Merrythought and others, and can easily be recognized by the pronounced triangular shape in the center of the stitching.

Farnells labeled its teddy bears using their name, country of origin, and the trade name "ALPHA TOYS."

Dark blue embroidered lettering on a creamy base indicates bears from this era.

ABOVE **This 1930s Merrythought – probably from the M line – has a new nose, but still has its wishbone button and foot label.**

MERRYTHOUGHT LTD. (1930)

Some of the early Merrythought bears have similar distinguishing features to bears produced by other firms, particularly Chad Valley. The two companies had their factories only a few miles apart, and one of the directors had previously worked for Chad Valley.

▌ Try to add to your collection Merrythought's early "M" line, or "Magnet" bear as it was also known.

▌ Merrythought also introduced a webbing pattern applied to the hand paws (a much flatter web formation than the earlier Farnell method and only has four "fingers.")

▌ Another distinguishing feature was the use of bright orange felt for pads, although of course other colors were also used.

▌ Merrythought adopted the use of a button in the ear for a few years. Shaped and formed similar to the one used by Chad Valley, but yellow with a wishbone trademark and overwritten "Hygienic – Merrythought – Toys." The button was usually attached to the left ear, but occasionally it can be found on the back of the bear.

▌ Fortunately, right from the start Merrythought adopted a labeling system of black lettering embroidered on a yellow background which was put on the sole of either foot. It was used until outbreak of World War II.

▌ "Bingie" was soon added to the line of bears (1931). This was a seated bear pattern and was so successful that it continued to be made for several years, until 1938. Some "Bingies" are dressed and had cloth bodies and limbs to save cost. The trademark label is found attached to the inside of the lower left leg.

LEFT **Two Merrythought "Bingies," a line produced 1931–1938, from the mid-1930s. The bears measure 10 and 13 inches.**

RIGHT **A Chiltern "Hugmee" from c. 1930, measuring 24 inches. The "Hugmee" was one of the finest quality British character bears ever produced and was made for more than 50 years from 1923 on.**

ABOVE **A Merrythought from the mid-1930s. It is an unusual color but still has its button and foot label (19 inches).**

H. G. STONE & CO. LTD. (1920)

The Chiltern line of "Hugmee" from the early 1920s and early 1930s are the real finds and the most desirable. Beautiful colored, fine-quality mohair was used, and filled with a mixture of excelsior and kapok, the bear truly lived up to its name "Hugmee."

▌ "Hugmees" had flat feet with velveteen pads reinforced with cardboard.

▌ Squeakers were inserted, but they are usually found inoperable.

ABOVE **A rare Chiltern bear from the late 1920s, measuring 22 inches. Note the distinctive "Hugmee" face and body.**

▌ Look for the large nose with its upturned, elongated outer stitching.
▌ Swing-type labels were attached, but you will be extremely lucky to find them still in place. They contained a circular trademark which can be helpful to identify the period. The very first bears (1923–6) have "Chiltern" at the top with an outline of rolling hills centrally

ABOVE **The "skater" bear was made by Chiltern in the late 1930s (13 inches). The muff and hat are original.**

located and overprinted with "Toys" and the trademark at the bottom.
▌ Subsequent labels from *circa* 1926, however, are similar but more decorative, with two houses in the left foreground but inscribed "trademark" (top), "Chiltern Toys" (center), and "Made in England" (bottom). These labels were used until well into the 1950s.
▌ Look for the "Cubby" (baby) line of bears introduced in 1930.

OTHER BRITISH MANUFACTURERS

EAST LONDON TOY FACTORY LTD. (1915) Continued with its "EALON" trademark teddy bears.

INVICTA TOYS Established in 1935; very little is known about this firm.

LINES BROTHERS/INTERNATIONAL MODEL AIRCRAFT CO. LTD. (1937) Produced the first "Pedigree" line of stuffed toys in 1937. In 1938, "Pedigree" advertised a teddy bear in its line, and this appears to be the first occasion it produced bears.

LOUIS GOLDBERG (1935) Offered the "cheapest grade of soft toys that have ever been produced in England" – brave words. The result was a fairly nondescript bear which will be hard to identify due to the millions of similar bears made at the time. Look for square shoulders, close-fitting legs, very pointed tapering arms, and a chest tag inscribed "Hygienic Toys" with the word "Teddy" centrally located.

THE SOUTH WALES TOY MANUFACTURING CO. (1917) Used the trade name "Madingland," but there are no known examples. The bears have unusually large, wrap-around ears which are set quite close together on top of the head, and unshaven faces with long extended mouths and a rather forlorn

ABOVE **Lines Brothers (Pedigree) bear from *c.* 1938 (21 inches). This line continued to be produced until the 1950s.**

look. Bodies and arms follow the German style, but the feet are in proportion quite small, round and bulbous, unlike the pre-World War I version which were very flat!

TAH TOYS LTD. (1919) Known to have made a line of bears in all sizes and colors, and although we have no examples, a 1919 advertisement indicates typically British-style rounded bodies, large heads, and very large floppy ears and enormously large feet. The noses on these bears were triangular with long vertical lines to short, horizontal mouths.

THE TEDDY TOY CO. (1916) Established during World War I; in the early 1920s introduced and patented (No. 133625) the "Softanlite" line of the lightest and softest teddy bears which they claimed to be the first! Its bears, which have not been positively identified, were illustrated in an early 1921 advertisement and appear to have large round faces, big ears, round button-style noses with downturned mouths. This company continued in production well into the 1950s.

GERMANY

GEBRÜDER BING (1908)

In 1920 Bing changed its name to Bing-Werke, and therefore the "GBN" button mark used previously was replaced by an orange button with the letters "BW" painted in black. The company closed in 1932.

▌ The button by now had been transferred from the body and attached to the outside of the arm.

▌ During the 1920s, many of the bears manufactured during the previous decade were reproduced with some changes to faces.

▌ Bing went out of business in 1932, and this of course makes its bears even more attractive.

▌ These bears can be found complete even with their button, which is an added bonus.

BELOW **A Bing-Werke bear from 1923/4, measuring 23 inches. These bears, with their long snouts, are very distinctive.**

BELOW **A Schuco compact bear from 1927/8 (3½ inches). This was one of the Piccolo line of novelty bears.**

SCHUCO (SCHREYER & CO) (1912)

The fashion of the day in the 1920s was for ladies to carry small clutch bags. Consequently, essential cosmetics had to be correspondingly small. How novel then that in 1942 Schuco should produce tiny little teddy bears which could contain all the essentials: perfume atomizer, compact, lipstick, and even a whiskey flask – for the gentlemen, of course! These bears were brightly colored, made from short bristly mohair attached around a metal body – a line known as "Piccolo." They remain a delightful find for any collector, but in very good condition they will not be cheap!

▌ The miniature mechanical wind-up tumbling bears, though lacking in bear character, are also great fun.

▌ The "Bellhop" produced from 1921 is a real character bear, and if it is found with its red tunic, black pants, pillbox hat, and leather bag all perfectly intact, it is a must for any collection.

▌ Without doubt one of the most sought after and treasured of all will be the "Yes-No" line. These bears can often be found in good condition because Schuco used only quality materials. The "Yes-No Clown" is the rarest of them all.

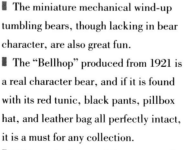

BELOW **A superb example of quality and character can be seen in this large Schuco from c. 1935 (height 20 inches). Note the three-pawed hands and feet typical of Schuco bears.**

MARGARETE STEIFF (1903)

At the time of the beginning of the red linen ear tag (1925–34), Steiff was producing some really nice, original bears; they are easily distinguishable from the earlier versions because their faces were now much slimmer, although still pointed, the back hump was now far less pronounced, and colored glass eyes were used. Do look for these bears; often they can be found in very good condition, but they can be rather expensive.

▌ Rare to find are the 1926 soft-filled "Teddy Clown" – multicolored brown frosted white mohair version made in 11 sizes, along with a plain colored "Clown" yellow bear. The latter bear was made with two different neck ruffs – one white with a red border, and the other white with a blue border, which is the rarer of the two.

▌ The "Petsy" range introduced in 1927 was offered in ten sizes and had the distinctive center-seam patterned head and was available in frosted mohair and

ABOVE **"Remembering Lou" – a Steiff from *c.* 1927/8 (height 16 inches). Blue-eye "Petsy" bears are very hard to find. Note the center seam and tipped mohair.**

BELOW LEFT **This lovely white Steiff from 1923/4 (height 23 inches). Steiff's line and style changed significantly after the mid-1920s.**

BELOW RIGHT **This Steiff was made after 1925 (*c.* 1925/6) as can be seen from the remains of the red tag attached to the button. The bear measures 24 inches.**

plain gold. Of these, the beautiful blue-eyed two-tone mohair bears are definitely the most sought.

▌ The "Teddy Baby" designed and produced in 1930 came in 11 sizes and was made in many different guises, some with open or closed mouths. These are very popular with collectors.

▌ Produced at the same time was the delightfully grinning bear called "Dicky." More usually, it was made from gold mohair in eight sizes and the rarer white version made in five sizes. Around 1936 a cheaper version with inset snout and large feet was made for a few years. You will be very lucky to find "Dicky" bears.

▌ The "Circus" bear, produced from 1936 until 1938, which had snap joints and a neck mechanism which meant the bear's limbs and head could be set to pose, remains one of the rarest bears from this whole era.

▌ Steiff also produced a considerable number of small bears which are popular with collectors.

OTHER GERMAN MANUFACTURERS

EDUARD CRAMER (1930) These hard-to-find bears from the early 1930s were clearly influenced by Steiff's "Teddy Baby" line and have similar features. A musical walking bear was based on the Steiff's "Clown" line with the same frosted mohair. One of the main features of these bears was the completely shaven snout. The bears had inset eyes, button-style noses, and partially open mouths, exposing soft pink felt tongues. The latter is unmistakably Cramer's most distinguishing feature, although the company also made closed-mouth bears.

GEBRÜDER HERMANN (1911) A family firm, under the control of Bernhard Hermann, producing bears in its Sonneberg factory. At the time, the bears had a simple swing tag attached to the upper chest, with the inscription "BEHA" on it "*BE*" taken from *Be*rnhard and "*HA*" from *Ha*mann. After 1930, "Beha" was displayed in small writing at the top with "Teddy" in large writing across the center. They are quite distinctive bears should you ever come across one, the main feature being the totally shaven inset snout with a triangular nose and short mouth. Possibly better known for the brown-frosted mohair bear produced in the mid-1920s. These should not be confused with the almost identical-style bear Hermann made 30 years later.

MAX HERMANN (1920) (LATER HERMANN-SPIELWAREN) A line of bears called series 112 in ten sizes was produced in the 1920s. They were quite different from their cousin's (Gebr. Hermann) creations, having unusual stand-up, pointed ears (almost cat-shaped) and long, inverted V-shaped mouths, giving them rather forlorn expressions. By the 1930s, the line had been increased with

series 111 (nine sizes), the main differences being the quality and color of fabric. These early models carried the trademark "MAHESO." Most bears were exported to the U.S.

H. JOSEF LEVEN & SPRENGER (1910) Made quite an extensive choice of bears. In the 1920s, they made eight different styles which expanded to 15 in the 1930s. All appear typically German, but otherwise details are limited.

GEBRÜDER SÜSSENGUTH (1925) Reputed to have produced several bear designs, but the best known was "Peter" bear with its movable eyes, tongue, and open mouth. Made in three sizes and colors, the most common of all is the brown-frosted mohair. It should have a white label with metal rim attached to its chest. It is still possible to find these

bears, and recently a small toy factory full of unopened boxed "Peters" was found.

AUSTRALIA

In general, the indigenous teddy-bear makers did not begin production until the late 1920s. One striking feature is the close resemblance between Australian bears and those produced by British manufacturers of the day.

BERLEX TOY PTY.
A Melbourne-based firm established in the 1930s.

▌ Apparently, the labels were attached to the underside of the left arm.

▌ Berlex bears from this era tend to be found well-worn.

EMIL TOYS

This firm came into being late in the 1930s and manufactured its bears in Victoria.

❚ A main distinguishing feature of these bears was their pugnacious appearance due to their large, round, permanently fixed heads set close to the shoulders, small ears, wide-set glass eyes, very distinctive broad noses with a pronounced upward elongated stitching, and long horizontal mouths.

ABOVE **This bear from Emil Toys, made in the late 1930s and measuring 16 inches, is recognizable by its fixed head.**

JOY TOYS PTY.

Australia's first teddy bear manufacturer was established in Melbourne in the late 1920s. But for some years, the firm struggled until *circa* 1935 when it started to produce Disney characters.

❚ Joy Toys bears from this era used quality mohair and were usually softly filled with cotton flock, except for the

ABOVE **This early Joy Toys bear from the 1930s, measuring 24 inches, is fully jointed, unlike many other Australian bears. It closely resembles British bears from the same era.**

head, which used excelsior, also used occasionally for the rest of the bear.

❚ A label, sewn across the center of the right foot rexine pad, was embroidered green on white "Joy-Toys made in Australia" (labels have also been found on the left foot).

❚ There is a close resemblance between Joy Toys and the Chiltern "Hugmee."

FRANCE

Probably of all the bears made during this period, these are the most difficult to authenticate. Perhaps the most distinctive features were the rather primitive exposed metal rods used to attach limbs, and short bristly mohair. Probably because of their inferior quality and their unhappy looks, French bears have been of little interest to collectors. However, they are now beginning to attract attention.

FADAP (1920)

Bears made by this firm (Fabrique Artistique d'Animaux en Peluche) are just beginning to appear and are recognizable by their distinctive red bordered tag, with a smaller overlapping circle at the bottom marked "FADAP," attached to the left ear with a metal button.

❚ This firm appeared to adopt the more conventional construction with concealed disk joints.

❚ The firm also produced teddy bears on wheels similar to Steiff's record series.

M. PINTEL FILS AND CIE

Early in the 1920s, it introduced bears.

❚ It used a small, round, molded, brass-colored button depicting two hugging bears and the letters "PF."

❚ Its bears had long tapering arms with long slender legs attached to a rather flat, almost shapeless body.

THIENNOT (1919–20)

Another French firm which is supposed to have started manufacturing bears following World War I. However, little information currently exists regarding these bears.

SWITZERLAND

HELVETIC (MID-1920s)

Manufacture began in the mid-1920s, but nobody can be quite sure about this maker's origins.

❚ The Helvetic range of musical bears are a must for any collector. The bears are quite distinctive, usually made of beautifully colored, long shaggy mohair with very appealing expressions.

❚ There is something rather American about these bears, so it may be that Swiss music boxes were shipped to the U.S. and inserted into locally made bears.

POSTWAR RECOVERY (1946–60)

CHAPTER 3

Ravaged by the two world wars and disrupted by serious economic problems, many of the world's teddy-bear manufacturers ceased to exist. A difficult time was in store for all the acknowledged quality toy manufacturers as they tried to pick up the pieces and re-establish themselves. They could not have foreseen that within three decades the world would drastically change beyond all recognition as the new technological age and throwaway society evolved. No longer were children encouraged to nurture their beloved favorite toy – toys soon became plentiful and children less considerate and far more demanding for the very latest toy! Cheap goods were the pre-requisite of the post-war baby boom.

It is surprising, therefore, that the most successful were the quality European manufacturers such as Steiff, Schuco, Hermann, Chiltern, and Chad Valley. Sadly, their success was short-lived as multinational conglomerate toy companies – usually American – swallowed up many competitors as they sought to control mass markets. No company was safe and all felt the threat of the big firms, as well as the threat of the continued rise of Japan as a major toy-producing nation.

To compound the problems for teddy-bear manufacturers, the American government introduced stringent new safety regulations in the late 1950s which soon spread to other countries.

The teddy bears which followed from the mid-1950s right through to the 1970s were certainly soft and cuddly, made to conform to international safety standards, and above all, cheap.

LEFT **This wonderful Chad Valley teddy *c.* 1950 is bidding farewell to an old friend – a Steiff *c.* 1905.**

COLLECTOR'S NOTEBOOK 1946–60

Unfortunately for collectors, the new safety rules so profoundly affected and restricted the design and manufacture of teddy bears that after about 1960 they are generally lacking in character and appeal.

U . S . A .

The mass-market conglomerates began to have their bears made in the cheap labor markets of the Far East. Inevitably, traditional teddy bear-makers found it difficult to compete.

CHARACTER NOVELTY CO.
The bears produced after the war and in the 1950s used the unusual technique of black button eyes applied to a white felt backing.
▌ This firm used a printed label bearing the name "Character" which appears to have been sewn into the bear's left ear.

GUND INC. (1906)
Gund made quite a variety of bears but tended to concentrate on producing stuffed toys based on Disney characters. Consequently, few distinctive teddy bears were produced.
▌ Fortunately, precise names of each product were included on their labels, which makes identification easy.

IDEAL TOY AND NOVELTY CO. (1903)
Like many of the post-war manufacturers, the quality of bears produced by this famous firm had gradually diminished over the years. As the company was now producing for the mass market, this is not surprising.
▌ During the 1950s, it produced a cute little teddy with molded vinyl face, hands, and feet. This method was quite popular among American firms during this time.

KNICKERBOCKER TOY CO.
Like so many others, this popular American firm was producing bears based on its pre-war designs except that it seemed to prefer the shaven inset muzzle rather like German firms. They produced some very nice, good-quality bears during the late 1940s and 1950s, but little else.

RIGHT **This Knickerbocker bear from the 1940s (height 20 inches) is one of the best postwar American teddies. Note the label on the chest.**

LEFT **The notable features of Character Novelty Co. bears of the late 1940s are the shape and the felt pads behind the eyes. (Height 19½ inches).**

BRITAIN

WENDY BOSTON (c. 1945)

Speak to anyone in Britain in his or her forties and they will probably tell you they were brought up on Wendy Boston bears produced during the 1950s and into the 1960s. The "Playsafe" nylon teddy could be thrown in the washing machine to emerge looking as good as new.

▋ These colorful one-piece bears came in all sizes and are now just beginning to be appreciated once again.

▋ Look for the bears with a pinkish-white printed satin trademark, usually sewn into the sole of the right foot. Even if the bear has been washed many times, you cannot mistake the label. Other manufacturers copied, but their bears were not the same.

▋ During the early 1950s, Wendy Boston also made conventional jointed mohair teddy bears. These would be a good find.

ABOVE **A representative variety of Wendy Boston "Playsafe" bears from the late 1950s and 1960s. Note that some bears have their labels on the right foot, which is normal, and some on the left.**

THE CHAD VALLEY CO. LTD. (1914)

Many of Chad's first bears after the war were based on the pre-war designs. Gradually, the wonderful character faces were sadly replaced by flat-faced, rather uninspiring teddy bears. Chad seemed to have lost its desire or perhaps ability to produce quality bears as the influence of the pre-war bears disappeared. With perhaps one or two exceptions, Chad bears from this era do not attract much attention.

RIGHT **A Chad Valley bear from c. 1950 measuring 28½ inches. This bear has the earlier Royal Warrant which reads "HM the Queen." It was changed in 1953 to read "HM Queen Elizabeth the Queen Mother."**

DEANS RAG BOOK CO. LTD. (1915)

A remarkable new line, based on real animals including a bear, was designed by Sylvia Wilgoss in 1955.

▌ Its molded face was overcovered with mohair, and it had molded rubber hands and feet.

▌ There was a black bear and a white bear (supposed to be a polar bear), and both are very scarce.

J.K. FARNELL & CO. LTD. (1908)

Almost the same can be said for Farnell except that some of the Farnell bears produced during early 1950s are worth seeking out. Look for the blue and red printed label with a shield, which was attached to bears made from 1940 to 1964. In 1964 to coincide with the company's moving to Hastings, Sussex, a plain printed label was used "This is a Farnell Quality Soft Toy made in Hastings, England." Unfortunately, the bears never really lived up to the slogan.

BELOW **A Deans bear from c. 1955 measuring 20 inches. The black versions of these "realistic" teddies are grizzly bears, and the off-white ones, as here, polar bears.**

MERRYTHOUGHT LTD. (1930)

The firm continued with similar designs from the late 1930s, but it really took the "Punkinhead" bear, followed by "Cheeky" to revive interest in Merrythought. Early versions of these particular bears should have the printed label with "Hygienic Toys" (center) rather than the wording "Ironbridge, Shrops" which appeared from 1957 on.

PEDIGREE SOFT TOYS LTD. (1937)

This was the name of a line of stuffed toys produced under the banner of Lines Brothers from 1937.

▌ The quality varied from good to poor, but the distinctive feature was a nose placed high on the face with a long lip extending down to the mouth.

▌ The bears were made in the London suburb of Merton until 1955 when production was transferred to Northern Ireland.

▌ Plastic noses were used extensively in the late 1950s.

ABOVE **These are two bears from Merrythought's popular "Cheeky" line. Made in the late 1950s, they measure 15 inches and 24 inches.**

RIGHT **This is probably the last real character bear produced by Farnells. The label on the side of the body sets the date of this bear to 1964/5. The height of the bear is 17½ inches.**

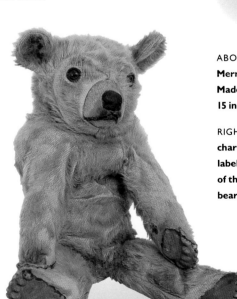

H.G. STONE & CO. LTD. (CHILTERN)

(1920) "Hugmee" bears still continued as the tour de force in the Chiltern line, and the 1950s bears are ones to look for.

▌ There were now facial changes with the introduction of the unshaven snout, but the general body construction and shape remained very much the same.

▌ Printed labels, blue on white, were now glued to the sole of the right foot. These often became detached, but if you look very carefully, you can usually see where they were.

▌ Red printed labels were also used on some teddy bears, but these, along with similar-style blue labels, were usually sewn into the seam at the side of the body.

▌ Plastic molded noses were used *circa* 1958, and the ears then applied were vertical floppy style.

▌ Other favorites are the Ting-a-Ling Bear (1953) and the musical Baby Bruin (1958). These are rather similar bears except the latter had fixed legs to enable it to stand upright.

OTHER BRITISH MANUFACTURERS

ACTON TOY CRAFT LTD. Produced the Twyford line of bears, which are really nice character bears but quite hard to find. Incidentally, Twyford bears often had red foot and hand pads.

LECO TOYS Whose bears are thought to be musical with a rather charming snub-nosed, upturned snout.

LEFRAY LTD. (1948) Established in 1948. Lefray bears were typically British for the period, except for a very unusual standing bear made with a fixed body and strange face.

RIGHT **A later (early 1960s) version of the Chiltern Hugmee, measuring 27 inches. The ears lie flat on the head, and the face is slightly more pointed than before.**

ABOVE **This musical standing bear made by Chiltern in 1959/60 measures 11½ inches. The nose is molded plastic.**

ABOVE **This Chiltern Hugmee was made c. 1956 and measures 21 inches. The basic shape of Hugmees had not changed.**

RIGHT **An unusual bear made by Lefray Ltd. in the mid-1950s (height 21 inches). It is made to stand on very short fixed legs, but the head and arms are jointed. The ears are lined with brown velvet, and the nostrils are red in color.**

S. OPPENHEIMER LTD. Produced teddy bears under the trademark "EMU" in 1950, distinguished by their triangular footpads.

PLUMMER AND WANDLESS & CO. LTD. Produced a line of teddy bears under the name of "Tinka-Bell."

W.T. CO. Produced a soft-bodied wind-up teddy in 1951 that danced and walked, and another magic eye (battery-operated) bear. These bears also had triangular foot pads.

GERMANY

GEBRÜDER HERMANN (1911)
Hermann continued to make similar bears to those produced in pre-war times, but also introduced a "Zotty" style around the same time as Steiff.

▌ Although these "Zottys" appear the same, the formation of the nose and mouth is quite different, the bear does not have a colored bib, and the eyes do not have felt backgrounds.

▌ Perhaps more collectible are the two-tone mohair bears produced during the mid-1950s, which closely resemble those produced before the war.

▌ Look for the green and silver rosette-style hanging chest tag introduced in 1952; if you find a bear with a circular pressed metal tag inscribed "Hermann – Teddy – Original," then you will know that bear was produced during the period 1941–51.

ABOVE **This popular bear by Gebrüder Hermann, made c. 1956 and measuring 16 inches, still has its green tag.**

ABOVE **This Gebr. Hermann bear is from c. 1953 and measures 12 inches. These may be hard to distinguish from Steiffs.**

SCHUCO (SCHREYER & CO.) (1912)

Schucho bears made immediately after World War II are the most sought-after of all those produced during Schuco's history.

❚ Without doubt, the star of the Schuco line was a version of the "Yes-No" bear called "Tricky." There was also a musical version of this bear. Look for one with its red rosette-style plastic chest tag inscribed "Schuco Tricky"; if it says "made in US Zone Germany" on the reverse side, it predates 1953.

❚ Another favorite, particularly if you can find her fully clothed, is the lovely "Yes-No" girl dressed in flowered dress and pinafore. Most notable is the fact that the head, hands, and feet were made of mohair and attached to an excelsior-filled fabric body, arms, and legs.

❚ Schuco also continued its line of metal-bodied miniatures; pre-war miniatures had felt feet applied, but these were not used after the war except, we believe, on one very early 1950s bear.

LEFT **A Schuco bear c. 1950 measuring 17½ inches. Schuco kept up its pre-war standards, but it is hard to find bears in such good condition.**

BELOW **This 1952 Steiff illustrates the gradual change in style between the late 1930s and the early 1950s. This bear measures 13 inches.**

BELOW **Steiff Zotties (l–r): 11 inches from 1956/7; 11 inches c. 1955; 11 inches c. 1970 and 8½ inches from the mid-1960s.**

MARGARETE STEIFF (1903)

If you look closely at the immediate post-war teddy bears, you can clearly see the relationship with those produced ten or twenty years before. The slender faces are still quite distinctively Steiff, but the new era demanded changes which even Steiff could not avoid.

▌ The 50th Anniversary bear produced in 1953 in three sizes called "Jackie" is likely to prove one of the best finds.

▌ The "Zotty" line of open-mouthed bears with their distinctive shaggy, frosted mohair and light-colored chests were introduced in 1951. They are great fun to collect, offering lots of variety, but always try for those complete with ear tag and chest label.

▌ Beware, however, because there were many lookalikes produced by other makers.

▌ The rarest of all "Zotty's" is the white one.

▌ Derivatives of the "Zotty" were the "Zulac Zotty," "Orsi," "Lully," and "Zooby," made during the mid-1950s and well worth considering.

BELOW **A Steiff bear from 1954/5 measuring 11 inches. In 1952, the original Steiff design became a little more rotund.**

OTHER GERMAN MANUFACTURERS

HERMANN-SPIELWAREN GMBH (1920)

The Hermann-Speilwaren company was formerly known as Max Hermann & Sohn with premises in Sonneberg. In 1947, Max Hermann changed the name of the firm to Hermann & Co Kg, which had premises in both Sonneberg and Coburg 20 miles away. In 1953, Max moved the whole firm from Sonneberg (in the Russian occupied zone) to Coburg where it has remained ever since. There were not, therefore, two different Hermann firms! Look for the early two-tone frosted mohair bear model 73. The firm used a green triangular pressed metal tag with a walking bear and a dog as its trademark.

PETZ COMPANY

There is much confusion and contradictory information about this company. Some authorities suggest the firm existed and was making bears as early as World War I, while others suggest they began after World War II. As yet, we cannot be sure. Most of the Petz bears you are likely to find can be positively identified if they have the distinctive white glass, red-lettered, round trademark tag attached to the chest; they are likely to be from about 1946 on.

▌ Other manufacturers known to have made bears during this period were: Clemens, Grisly Spielwaren, Althans KG, Anker, Baweku GmbH, Baumann & Kienel KG, EBO, Heunec, and Hugo Koch.

AUSTRALIA

BERLEX TOY PTY. (1930s)

Quite when this firm started making bears is not clear, although it had been in operation since the 1930s. We suspect it was probably some time in the 1950s, because the bears are typical of that era employing cheaper quality mohair.

▌ They adopted the fixed head style which was popular among many Australian bear-makers.

▌ Look for the red printed on white label attached to either arm and triangular stitched noses, which Berlex favored.

BELOW **The head on this 1950s Berlex bear is fixed, but the limbs are jointed. Note the triangular nose and the label on the left arm. (Height 20 inches).**

BELOW **A bear from the Australian company Emil Toys. It was made in the 1950s and measures 20 inches. Despite having only one eye, this fixed-head mohair bear will appeal to a great many collectors. Note the elongated outer stitching on the nose.**

RIGHT **This attractive bear was made c. 1960 and measures 30 inches. Although made from a woolen-blend plush, it has a great character. Note the label on the right foot.**

EMIL TOYS (LATE 1930S)

The bears made by this firm were remarkably similar to those made by Joy Toys, except Emil Toys bears always seem to lack any claw markings.

▊ Look for the label on the back or arm with a large letter "E" with a teddy bear on it.

JAKAS (1954)

Based in Melbourne, Jakas began bear-making in 1954. The firm made a wide variety of stuffed toys including teddy bears and usually used a black printed on fawn-colored silk label sewn on the right foot pad.

JOY TOYS PTY. (LATE 1920S)

Postwar Australian makers, including Joy Toys, still followed similar design concepts to the British.

▊ Although mohair had been extensively used, it was now replaced more and more by cheap synthetic plushes. The soft cotton flock filling was also dropped in favor of synthetic foam filling. The problem with the latter is it deteriorates and crumbles easily.

▊ Both the elongated, outer stitched nose and the green printed on white label were retained in postwar production by Joy Toys.

BELOW **A typical Australian bear from Joy Toys. Made in the 1960s and measuring 15 inches, it is filled with foam rubber.**

LINDEE TOYS (LATE 1940s)
Established in Sydney during the late war years, it produced a variety of typically Australian teddy bears.

▌ During its early period it made a rather attractive musical bear with a distinctive molded rubber nose and unusual teardrop-shaped rexine pads.

▌ A trademark sewn to the right foot was an unusual red painted on white seated deer with the words "Lindee Toys" inscribed inside.

Other manufacturers known to have made bears during this period were L.J. Sterne Doll Co. of East Malvern, Victoria, and Parker Toys of Brunswick, Victoria.

ABOVE **An appealing bear from Lindee Toys, made in the 1950s and measuring 20 inches. Note the molded rubber nose and tear-shaped rexine foot pads.**

RIGHT **This foam-filled Verna bear was made in the 1950s and measures 30 inches. Note the kidney-shaped black felt nose and embroidered mouth.**

VERNA (LATE 1940s)
Although this firm was established in 1941, it seems highly likely that due to wartime trade restrictions, it did not start manufacturing bears until around 1948.

▌ Verna bears have a strong British influence, but look for the nose made of pieces of kidney-shaped felt.

▌ Foam-rubber molding techniques were used for the heads, bodies, and limbs, to which the fabric was applied.

▌ Verna bears were marked by a red embroidered on white label.

OTHER MANUFACTURERS

BERG This Austrian bear-maker began immediately after World War II and marked its bears with a label reading "BERG" sewn into the ear on the body. Later this was changed to a red heart-shaped trademark sewn into the chest.

FETCHER Immediately after World War II, this firm began manufacture in Graz, Austria, and an open-mouthed bear was a prominent feature of their line. Easily distinguishable by their very large round heads, inset snouts, and very large ears which usually had different colored lined inner ears placed at the top of the heads. The Fetcher label was sewn to the outside of the bear's right ear. Quite often, red-colored eyes appear to have been used.

MUTZI (M.C.Z.) This Swiss firm based in Zurich made a wide variety of teddy bears, which are very like German bears in appearance. It used a round metal button with the emblem of a teddy bear with "Mutzi M.C.Z." on a red painted base. So far as we can tell, Felpa AG and Mutzi were the same company.

THE AGE OF SPECIAL EDITION BEARS

CHAPTER 4

After nearly two decades – the 1960s and 1970s – when very few bears of serious interest to collectors were produced, 1980 marked the start of a new and exciting era. It was Margarete Steiff GmbH which was again to dominate, reaffirming its position as leading manufacturer of quality stuffed toys and teddy bears.

LEFT One of the best contemporary Steiffs – the first of the British Collector's series is a 1989 replica of a 1907 bear (height 24 inches).

ABOVE This is a full set of the delightful 1909 replicas issued by Steiff between 1983 and 1988. The smaller and larger bears were issued only to the United States.

RIGHT A wonderful mohair bear by Little Folk from 1982 measuring 22 inches is also available as 12 inch and was only produced for about 2 years.

MANUFACTURERS SPECIALIZING IN LIMITED EDITIONS

U.S.A.

BEARLY THERE INC. (1976)

Started in 1976 by Linda Spiegel Lohre. The original bears were rather traditional, but since *circa* 1985, the bears have shown a close affinity to the "Artist"-type bear. Bearly There bears continue to be extremely popular all over the world.

NORTH AMERICAN BEAR CO. (1979)

Barbara Isenberg created this company in 1979, but the introduction of the Very Important Bear line (V.I.B.) in 1980 was what really caught the collector's eye. Based on famous celebrities, the range included Amelia Bearheart, Abearheim Lincoln, Bearlie Chaplin, Bearilyn Monroe, and Elizabear Taylor with Richard Bearton, based on the film *Cleopawtra*.

▌ In 1983, it produced an edition of "Hug," the famous character bear by Ted Menten.

▌ Another hugely successful line was the "Vanderbear" series and the "Muffy" series.

▌ Initially preferred by American collectors, these bears are now appreciated in other parts of the world.

ROBERT RAIKES ORIGINALS (1982)

These charming and funny little bears are quite distinctive with their wooden character faces.

▌ The first bears were produced by Robert Raikes' own hand in 1982, but since around 1984 all his design creations have been manufactured by Applause.

▌ The pre-Applause bears are among the most sought-after of all contemporary bears, and Raikes has a tremendous following. However, those first Applause-made bears are also much in demand (the first edition of 7,500 was sold out in three weeks).

▌ Of the original bears made by Raikes' own hands, the first one is simply called "Woody Bear" and subsequent designs – "Panda Woody Bear" and "Tyrone Woody Bear" (Scotsman) – are the most in demand and rather expensive.

▌ The first series, limited to 7,500 each and issued in Autumn 1985 by Applause, included Sebastian (5445), Huckle Bear (5446), Rebecca (5447), Bentley (5448), Eric (5449), and Chelsea (5551).

BRITAIN

CANTERBURY BEARS (1981)

John and Maude Blackburn began serious manufacture of bears in 1981 and have grown from a small family group to a medium-sized company. Canterbury has produced large quantities of standard-line bears in addition to limited editions especially for collectors, all of which are handmade by a loyal and dedicated workforce.

▌ The Blackburns are great favorites on the American personal appearance circuit. Since 1991, they have collaborated with Gund Inc. of America to make a very special line of collectible limited editions for the U.S.

RIGHT **"Hug," from the North American Bear Co., was designed by Ted Menten and measures 18 inches. It was one of their earliest successes – *c*. 1983.**

ABOVE **"Rosie" by Canterbury Bears was made in 1993. She was designed by Maude and John Blackburn, two leading designers of both special editions and standard lines. She measures 21 inches.**

ABOVE **Canterbury Bear's 10th anniversary bear (100/500) from 1991 (23 inches) embraces the special edition "Swallow" (1/25) made in 1993 (24 inches).**

LEFT **This attractively costumed plush bear "heading for the hills" was the result of a collaboration between Lakeland Bears, who designed the outfits, and Little Folk c. 1991. The bear measures 23½ inches.**

DEANS RAG BOOK CO. LTD. (1915)
(NOW THE DEANS COMPANY (1903)

This is another British company which realized the importance of the collectors' market, when in 1981 it produced bears for the U.S. based on Norman Rockwell drawings. It has continued to manufacture collectible bears, and in the past few years its line has substantially improved.

LITTLE FOLK (1980)

From the outset in 1980, Little Folk realized there was greater potential in the U.S., where most of its bears were exported. The very early designs used mohair, but this meant the bears were probably too expensive, and cheaper acrylic plush was successfully introduced *circa* 1982. This same line is produced today and much in demand.

■ A 2,000 limited edition bear Sebastian (1987) and 500 No Johnathon's (1990) have also been produced with collectors in mind. We have a special place in our hearts for Little Folk bears because they were the very first contemporary bears we sold.

MERRYTHOUGHT LTD. (1930)

In 1982 Merrythought decided to introduce a line of limited edition bears, usually based on their old designs, for the U.S. market. Recently, several new designs have been added, including those inspired by John Axe (author of *The Magic of Merrythought*) and others based on the drawings of the English illustrator, Prue Theobalds.

HOUSE OF NISBET (1978)

Of all the contemporary manufacturers, the House of Nisbet under the leadership of Jack Wilson was probably the most adventurous. He cultivated an extremely fruitful business relationship with the amazing Peter Bull, resulting in the introduction of the "Bully Bear" line, and the delightful edition of 12 "Zodiac" bears, based on a book by Pauline McMillan and Peter Bull. It was a great loss to the teddy-bear world when Jack decided to retire in 1989, and the House of Nisbet was taken over by Dakin.

■ "Delicatessan" ("Aloysius"), another of Peter Bull's bears, is without equal and incidentally was directly responsible for the introduction of distressed mohair which artists have since found so helpful.

ABOVE **"Delicatessan" (number 1031 of 2500) from the House of Nisbet, c. 1987, measures 25 inches. This limited edition is now rather hard to find and is a must for any collector.**

THE NISBET CELEBRITY
COLLECTION

Hedda Hair bear from 1989 (16 inches).

The following bears, produced in the Nisbet Celebrity Collection, were limited to 5,000 of each design.

Yetta Bear, Eric-Jon Bear, Maybe and Wizard, all by Carol-Lynn Rössell Waugh ● Little Brown Bear by Johnny Gruelle ● Pearly King Bear by Doris and Terry Michaud ● Uncle Wiggily by Mabel R. Garis ● The Bell Hop Bear and The Clown Bear by April Whitcomb ● Yes-No Bear, based on the Schuco method ● Sir Freddie Farthing by Ted Menten ● Precious the Paper Doll Bear by Peggy Jo Rosamond ● Mr. Do-it-all Bear by Linda Mullins ● The Hedda Hair Bear by Lillian Rohaly ● The Anything Bear by Rosemary Volpp ● Theodore B. Bear and Victoria Bear, both by Beverley Port ● Red Mittens Bear by Pat Schoonmaker ● Grinnee Bearit by Lucy Major ● Gyles Bear by Gyles Brandreth ● Drum Major Bear by Dee Hockenberry ● and Bentley Bear by Dakin.

Although listed in Nisbet's 1990 catalog, the Jim Ownby Tribute Bear by Peggy Maxwell was apparently never produced.

❙ The "Nisbet Celebrity" collection was an inspired move by the astute Jack who had been quick to realize that there were other "celebrities" in the rapidly expanding Teddy Bear collecting fraternity. In 1987 he invited well-known people to have a bear made in their name or asked artists to design a special bear.

GERMANY

GEBRÜDER HERMANN (1911)

This small family firm, consistently one of Germany's mainstream producers, entered the new specialist production market in 1984. Like many other established firms, it has produced bears based on its earlier designs that have been well received by collectors worldwide.

❙ The "Anniversary" bear (1986), "Designer" bear (1991), "Berlin Wall" bear (1991), and "Unification" bear (1991) are perhaps the best-known.

ABOVE **A limited edition replica of a 1930s bear from Gebrüder Hermann. It was issued to commemorate Helen Sieverling's efforts to expand teddy bear collectors' knowledge.**

BELOW **The "Designer" bear, 1991, measuring 23 inches, shows the character and quality of the limited edition bears produced by Gebrüder Hermann.**

MARGARETE STEIFF (1903)

Spurred on by the need for a fresh approach to fight off the threat of cheap imports, Steiff introduced a special edition teddy bear in 1980 to commemorate the 100th anniversary of the company. Its success enabled the firm to implement state of the art production methods to reproduce the originals kept in the Steiff museum, which had also opened that year, as faithfully as possible, modern materials permitting.

▌ Steiff regularly made exclusive limited editions for major department stores worldwide and also produced editions for Disney World and Disneyland Conventions held annually in the U.S.

▌ Many, but by no means all, of the Steiff replica bears have appreciated in value, some substantially, which may be an inducement to some collectors.

▌ So many special limited editions of bears have been issued that a reference chart of those produced by Steiff until 1993 is given on page 45. Only limited editions carrying white tags have been included. Although some absolutely wonderful yellow-tag (standard production) bears were produced, it is impossible to list them, too.

▌ Many of the yellow tags are highly collectible, and some can be rather expensive; perhaps the most desirable are the early "Mr. Cinnamon" bears made in three sizes and several ranges of the "Margaret Strong" bears produced in the mid-1980s.

BELOW **Steiff's 1990 replica of the world-famous "Happy," looking as she would have done when new in 1926. She measures 26 inches.**

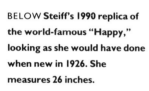

BELOW **One of five sizes of (unlimited) "Margaret Strong" gold bears introduced by Steiff in 1982. (23½ inches).**

STEIFF LIMITED EDITION TEDDY BEARS

KEY TO SCARCITY FACTOR

1–3	currently available and easy to find
4–5	moderately easy to find
6–8	relatively difficult to find
9–10	very rare and expensive

NOTE: Until 1991, the last two numbers of a product code indicate size in centimeters. The EAN number, a European standard, was then introduced.

N/A = not applicable   W/W = worldwide

ABOVE **"Jubilee" or "Papa" bear was the first modern limited edition, produced in 1980 (height 17 inches).**

YEAR OF PRODUCTION		REPLICA PRODUCT CODE	DESCRIPTION	QUANTITY	SCARCITY FACTOR
ORIGINAL	REPLICA				
1903	1980	0153/43	JUBILEE BEAR, but commonly known as PAPA BEAR	11,000 W/W (6,000 German certificate, 5,000 to U.S.A., English certificate)	9–10
1903	1981	0155/38	MAMA and BABY SET (Mama 16 inches, Baby 6 inches)	8,000 U.S.A.	9
N/A	1982	0203/00	ORIGINAL TEDDY WHITE SET	2,000 U.S.A.	9
N/A	1982	0204/17	TEA PARTY SET (4 dressed bears with tea set and scene)	10,000 U.S.A.	6–7
1905	1982/83	0150/32	RICHARD STEIFF GRAY TEDDY BEAR	Unnumbered. No certificate but tied-on booklet is signed. Estimates vary from 11,000 to 20,000 W/W	8
N/A	1983	0210/22	TEDDY ROOSEVELT COMMEMORATIVE SET or NIMROD or CAMP FIRE (4 small dressed bears with scene)	10,000 U.S.A. (Note: many sets were broken up and bears sold separately)	7
1904	1983	0160/00	MARGARET STRONG CHOCOLATE SET (4 different bears 7 inches, 10½ inches, 12¾ inches, and 17 inches)	2,000 U.S.A.	8

RIGHT **The "Circus Dolly" bear, issued in 1987, was made in four colors. It was first distributed in the U.S., followed by the rest of the world.**

LEFT **"Dicky" was produced in 1985 in a very large limited edition of 20,000, but its collectibility is now increasing (height 13 inches).**

RIGHT **The delightful "Teddy Clown" was made in 1986 and measures 13 inches. As with all Steiff collector's bears, it is handmade from the finest quality mohair.**

ABOVE **This small gray "Richard Steiff" was made in 1982/3 and measures 13 inches. It was based on Richard Steiff's prototype and is a great favorite with collectors.**

YEAR OF PRODUCTION ORIGINAL	REPLICA	REPLICA PRODUCT CODE	DESCRIPTION	QUANTITY	SCARCITY FACTOR
1904	1984	0156/00	MARGARET STRONG CINNAMON SET (4 different bears 7 inches, 10½ inches, 12¾ inches, 17 inches)	2,000 U.S.A.	8–9
1894	1984	0082/20	ROLY-POLY BEAR	9,000 W/W	4–5
1906	1984	0162/00	GIENGEN TEDDY SET (Mother 12½ inches with Baby in Cradle 4 inches)	16,000 W/W	6–7
N/A	1984	4003 (Large Set)	GOLDILOCKS & 3 BEARS Papa Bear 13 inches, Mama 12 inches, Baby 9½ inches. Doll by Susan Gibson	2,000 U.S.A.	7
N/A	1984	0225/42	OPHELIA BEAR from *Ophelia's World* by Michelle Durkson-Clise	U.S.A. Limited by time production (Note: Button but no tag)	7
1930	1985	0172/32	DICKY BEAR	20,000 W/W	6
1905	1985	0085/12	BEAR ON WHEELS	12,000 W/W	5
N/A	1985	4004 (Smaller Set)	GOLDILOCKS & 3 BEARS Papa Bear 9 inches, Mama 7 inches, Baby 5 inches, and doll	5,000 U.S.A.	6–7
1904	1985	0158/25 0158/31 0158/41	MARGARET STRONG WHITE (leather pads) (leather pads) (leather pads)	2,000 U.S.A.	8
1904	1986	0158/50	MARGARET STRONG WHITE (leather pads) Large	750 U.S.A.	9–10
1926	1986	0170/32	TEDDY CLOWN	10,000 W/W	7
1953	1986/7	0190/25	JACKIE BEAR (medium-size)	10,000 W/W	6–7
1913	1987	0164/31 0164/32 0164/33 0164/30	CIRCUS DOLLY BEARS yellow green violet pale yellow (Note: blue and red also shown in catalog but not produced)	5,000 U.S.A. initially, then W/W	6–7 6 6 9

BELOW **"Teddy Rose,"** a center seam replica, was made in 1987 and measures 16 inches and has many fans among collectors.

RIGHT **"Jackie,"** a reproduction of the 1953 anniversary bear, was first made in 1988 and is shown here in all the sizes so far issued.

YEAR OF PRODUCTION		REPLICA PRODUCT CODE	DESCRIPTION	QUANTITY	SCARCITY FACTOR
ORIGINAL	REPLICA				
1905	1987	0163/19	TEDDY CLOWN, JR.	3,000 U.S.A. with white tags (Note: 2,000 also issued with yellow tags)	8–9
1925	1987	0171/41	TEDDY ROSE	10,000 W/W	6–7
1907	1987	0227/33	SCHNUFFY	Limited by time production issued to U.S.A. but later about 300 released into U.K. (undressed) (Note: Button, no tag)	7
N/A	1987	0131/00	THREE BEARS IN A TUB butcher, baker, and candle-stick maker in tub	1,800 U.S.A.	7–8
N/A	1988	0227/33	BABY OPHELIA	Unstated limit U.S.A. Only *Button* in ear	6
N/A	1988	0120/10	BEAR BANDSMAN (Circus series)	5,000 U.S.A.	5–6

YEAR OF PRODUCTION		REPLICA PRODUCT CODE	DESCRIPTION	QUANTITY	SCARCITY FACTOR
ORIGINAL	REPLICA				
1953	1988	0190/35	JACKIE BEAR (large)	4,000 W/W	5–6
1908	1988	0155/18	ROLY-POLY BEAR	3,000 U.S.A.	7
1908	1988	0174/46	WHITE MUZZLE BEAR (medium-size)	5,000 U.S.A.	7–8
1907	1988	0173/40	BLACK BEAR (with leather nose)	4,000 W/W	8–9
1924	1988	0132/24	'WIG-WAM' BEAR 2 small bears and pull-along seesaw	4,000 W/W	5–6
1907	1989	0174/61	BRITISH COLLECTORS SERIES BEAR (1st)	2,000 U.K.	9–10
1939	1989	0135/20	BABY BEAR ON TROLLEY	4,000 W/W	4–5
1931	1989	0130/28	BEAR ON ALL FOURS	4,000 U.S.A.	6
1908	1989 reissued 1991 (U.S.A.)	0158/17	SNAP-APART BEAR	5,000 W/W	5–6
N/A	1989	0175/19	TEDDY BEAR RINGMASTER	7,000 U.S.A.	4–5
N/A	1989	0163/20	CLOWN TEDDY From golden age of the circus series	5,000 U.S.A.	5

LEFT **This black bear (issued in 1987) caused a great furore when issued in Britain; because of small numbers, its price trebled within a year (height 15¾ inches).**

BELOW **This "Snap-Apart" bear issued in 1989 measures 6¾ inches.**

LEFT **The "Petsy Brass" replica was issued in 1989 and measures 13¾ inches.**

RIGHT **This is the reproduction of the blue "Bi-color Petsy" issued in 1989. It measures 19¾ inches.**

YEAR OF PRODUCTION		REPLICA PRODUCT CODE	DESCRIPTION	QUANTITY	SCARCITY FACTOR
ORIGINAL	REPLICA				
1927	1989	0181/35	PETSY BRASS	5,000 W/W	6
1953	1989	0190/17	JACKIE BEAR	12,000 W/W	4
1927	1989	0180/50	BICOLOR PESTY CENTER SEAM	5,000 U.S.A.	6–7
1908	1989	0174/60	WHITE MUZZLE BEAR (large)	2,650 U.S.A.	9–10
1908	1990	0174/35	WHITE MUZZLE BEAR (small)	6,000 W/W	5
1926	1990	0169/65	HAPPY ANNIVERSARY REPLICA	5,000 W/W	8–9
1925	1990	0171/25	TEDDY ROSE (small)	8,000 W/W	5
N/A	1990	0177/19	TEDDY BABY FOOD SELLER (Circus series)	5,000 U.S.A.	4–5
1955	1990	0188/25	TEDDY WITH NECK MECHANISM	4,000 W/W	5–6
1909	1990	0164/29	SOMERSAULT BEAR	5,000 W/W	6–7
1906	1990	0174/33	BRITISH COLLECTORS SERIES BEAR (No. 2)	3,000 U.K.	5–6
1913	1990	0116/25	RECORD TEDDY (on wheels)	4,000 W/W	7–8
N/A	1991	650529 (EAN)	TEDDY BABY TICKET SELLER (Circus series)	5,000 U.S.A.	4–5
1903	1991	404108 (EAN)	35 PB REPLICA (20-inch) (in U.S.A. often referred to as "Baerle" bear)	6,000 W/W	8

Year of Production		EAN Numbers Used	Description	Quantity	Scarcity Factor
Original	Replica				
1926	1991	407215	Baby Happy Anniversary (16 inches) (Note: Box incorrectly states 5,000 limit, but certificate is correct)	6,000 W/W	4–5
1912	1991	406096	British Collectors Series Black Bear (No. 3) (13 inches)	3,000 U.K.	5–6
1908	1991	406119	Dark Brown Muzzle (14 inches)	5,000 U.S.A.	4–5
1913	1991	400704	Record Teddy Rose (on wheels)	4,000 W/W	3–4
1931	1991	408113	Yellow Teddy Baby (6 inches)	5,000 U.S.A.	4
1931	1991	408114	Yellow Teddy Bear (12½ inches)	5,000 U.S.A. (a few later released to U.K.)	4
N/A	1991	650529	Teddy Baby Ticket Seller (Circus series)	5,000 U.S.A.	4
1930s	1991	606106	Teddy Baby Watch Set (1st Issue – complete stand, bear, and 13 watches)	2,000 W/W	8 Complete Set
1930s	1992	606304	Teddy Baby Watch Set (2nd Issue – complete stand, bear, and 13 watches)	4,000 W/W	6–7

LEFT **This group of white muzzled bears was issued between 1988 and 1990. The larger one (23½ inches) is extremely hard to find. The other sizes are 13¾ inches and 18 inches. Most collectors remove the muzzles.**

RIGHT **The 35PB replica was issued in 1991. It reproduces the string joints and sealing wax nose (height 19½ inches).**

BELOW **This somersault or "Purzel" bear was issued in 1990 and measures 11½ inches. It uses a wind-up mechanism.**

LEFT **The British Collector's series always produces attractive bears. This brown bear was issued in 1993 (height 24 inches).**

RIGHT **Another in the British Collector's series issued in 1992 and measuring 16 inches.**

YEAR OF PRODUCTION		EAN NUMBERS USED	DESCRIPTION	QUANTITY	SCARCITY FACTOR
ORIGINAL	REPLICA				
1911	1992	406645	BRITISH COLLECTORS SERIES WHITE BEAR (No. 4) (Sometimes referred to as LOUISE in the U.K.) (16 inches)	3,000 U.K.	4–5
1928	1992	407482	YELLOW MUSICAL BEAR (16 inches)	8,000 W/W	3–4
1930	1992	407550	WHITE DICKY BEAR (10 inches)	9,000 W/W	3
1930	1992	407574	WHITE DICKY BEAR (13 inches)	7,000 W/W	3
1912	1992	406805	SMALL BLACK BEAR (16 inches)	7,000 W/W	3–4
1912	1992	406774	"OTTO" 1st ISSUE NEW U.S.A. COLLECTORS SPECIAL (16 inches)	5,000 U.S.A.	3–4
1974	1992	400872	SEESAW BEAR AND MONKEY (on wheels)	4,000 W/W	3
N/A	1992	038006 (WO38006)	NOAH'S ARK WITH MR. AND MRS. NOAH (8 inches) BEARS WITH BAMBOO ARK (Note: Wooden ark alternative offered in U.S.A.)	8,000 W/W	4
1905	1993	404207	BARLE 35 PAB (14 inches)	6,000 W/W	3–4
1926	1993	400919	UR TEDDY (8 inches)	4,000 W/W	1

Year of Production Original	Replica	EAN Numbers Used	Description	Quantity	Scarcity Factor
1951	1993	408458	Musical Teddy (14 inches)	5,000 W/W	2
1907	1993	406010	Teddy Bear Brown 1907 (28 inches)	5,000 W/W	4–5
1930	1993	407512	Teddy Baby Dressed Girl	7,000 W/W	1
1930	1993	407529	Teddy Baby Dressed Boy	2,000 W/W	1
1907	1993	406065	British Collectors Series Large Brown (No 5) (24 inches)	3,000 W/W	4
1903	1993	650574	Alice 2nd Issue U.S.A. Special Collectors Series	5,000 W/W	3
N/A	1993	038327	Bear Set for Ark Series (2 bears)	8,000 W/W	2
1929	1992/93	420016	Steiff 1st Issue Club Bear Blue Teddy Baby (11 inches)	approx 7,500 issued outside U.S.A.	Available only to Steiff Collector Club members
N/A	1993/94	420023	Steiff 2nd Issue Club Bear Teddy Clown (11 inches)	issued outside U.S.A.	Available only to Steiff Collector Club members
N/A	1993/94	420801	Steiff USA 1st Issue Club Bear – Sam	issued only in U.S.A.	Available only to Steiff Collector Club members U.S.A. only

LEFT The first U.S.A. Steiff Collector's Club issue in 1994 was a bear called "Sam" (height 11 inches).

RIGHT The European Collector's Club was introduced in 1993 and has been a huge success. The "Blue Teddy Baby" (11 inches) was an exclusive issue to club members.

THE ERA OF THE TEDDY BEAR ARTIST

CHAPTER 5

The trouble in trying to define the term "teddy bear artist" is that this is such a contentious and emotive subject, you inevitably alienate some people. Probably above all else, the major feature which distinguishes the real teddy bear artist from all other crafts people or bear-makers is the ability to create, without the conscious influence of others, a teddy bear of distinctive quality and character. It is not just a matter of good workmanship, however desirable this may be; the design concept must be original with a clear esthetic quality and style.

Many people are perfectly competent bear-makers and their workmanship is consistent and precise, but they are simply incapable of instilling life in a bear, or,

LEFT **Deborah Canham is one of Britain's best artists. These delightful circus bears (2 inches) were made in 1993.**

RIGHT **Jo Greeno (U.K.) created "Miss Marple," based on Agatha Christie's famous detective, in 1993 (height 19 inches). Jo specializes in wonderful characters from the past. They are usually kept to small limited editions or are one-off designs.**

LEFT **"Wizard" by Brenda Davey (U.S.A.) c. 1993. He measures 5 inches and is typical of her Fantasy style. Diverse in size and inspiration, these bears are usually limited editions or one-of-a-kind.**

LEFT "Lady Margaret" was made by one of America's top artists, Marcia Sibol, in 1991 (height 33 inches) especially for the authors. She is the gossip columnist of the *Teddy Bear Times*!

RIGHT **Diane Gard (U.S.A.)** based "Billy Ray" on an American football hero. He was made exclusively for the 1992 Walt Disney World Doll and Teddy Bear Convention.

ABOVE **Janet Clark has been making bears seriously for three years and is now one of Britain's top artists. "Loving" was made in 1994.**

RIGHT **"Bearlin the White Wizard" by Kathryn Riley was created in 1993. Amazingly, he was only her third bear!**

as our old friend Steve Schutt often says, "giving the bear a soul." An artist bear must be instantly recognizable as the work of a particular creator, just as most people can easily distinguish the work of, say, Van Gogh from a painting by old Aunt Mabel!

All artists have to be innovators; otherwise, their work becomes mundane, rather than inspirational and a teddy that we simply must own. A true teddy bear artist will possess a wide-ranging repertoire, be adventurous and not afraid to disregard convention, and instinctively be able to produce everything from classical to whimsical and occasionally unusual designs. The artist will seek out new materials, apply new techniques or concepts, and constantly diversify his or her designs, rarely being perfectly content with the result.

Where did bear artistry begin? The true origins of the teddy bear artist are somewhat obscure, although we only have to go back to the 1970s in the United States to find who were the guiding spirits and true pioneers of the movement.

Many of the early craft bear-makers and their successors were largely influenced by two English people. One was Margaret Hutchings, a reporter for one of Britain's leading newspapers, who in 1964 wrote the definitive teddy bear-making manual, *The Book of the Teddy Bear*. The other was of course Peter Bull.

LEFT "Marisa Bearensen" was made by Diane Gard in 1988 (height 24 inches). She was created for Ted Menten's parody of *Harper's Bazaar*. "Marisa" is dressed in her Yves St. Bearant gown.

RIGHT "Jenny-Lynn" was made by Carol-Lynn Rössel Waugh in 1993 (height 20 inches). Carol-Lynn is a top artist in addition to being a prolific writer and an authority on teddy bear artistry. She has also designed bears for manufacturers.

The first teddy bear artist was the American, Beverley Port. From the 1970s, Beverley guided and taught many of the current teddy bear artists. She had broken free from the traditional restraints and prejudices which had restricted her as a doll artist to pursue her new interest in teddy bear-making, encouraging a great many others by her example. She is recognized as the "mother" of teddy bear artistry.

In 1980, the Americans Alan and Peggy Bialosky produced their book *Teddy Bears Catalog* which provided added impetus and stimulus to those involved with teddy bears.

Carol-Lynn Rössell Waugh, herself an ex-doll maker, was one of the early disciples of this new movement. An art historian, she became a prominent authority on the subject and was probably the person who coined the term "teddy bear artist." She has written extensively over the years promoting the work of artists, and has herself produced many fine bears, as well as designing for major manufacturers.

Another artist who was an undoubted inspiration and influence on the movement, not least because of his own designs, was Ted Menten. A photographer and author, his many wonderful teddy bear books have inspired others. His outrageous parody of *Harpers Bazaar* entitled *Teddy's Bearzaar* provided a unique

opportunity for the invited artists to make special bears displaying their tremendous flair. The bears replaced the usual female models in the advertisements and articles to provide an absolutely wonderful, whimsical, and funny book that has helped to open new horizons and, most important, to validate artists and their bears as a highly collectible commodity.

ABOVE "Elfinbeary Peach" (14/100) illustrates Joan Woessner's versatility and creativity and confirms her position as a top American artist (1992).

LEFT **Anne Cranshaw's (U.S.A.) "Casco Bear"** (1993, 14½ inches) is a captivating little bear created for *Teddies of the World '93*.

RIGHT **"Bear and his Friend Grin it"** was made by **Karin and Howard Calvin (U.S.A.)** as a limited edition (1988, height 15 inches).

Around 1982–3 in the U.S. many aspiring people became attracted to bear-making, and some with undoubted qualities began to emerge and develop their skills. Teddy bear shows were also being established, which gave prominence to a new generation of bear-makers – real artists who brought to the art not only new and invigorating design concepts but a positive desire to create an artistic group or community. Among the many who became idealistically involved were Steve Schutt, Diane Gard, Joan Woessner, Anne Cranshaw, and Denis Shaw, who by their example epitomized integrity and strong ethical principles which bear artists were to find invaluable in the years ahead.

The foundations were laid for these instigators, and others, to encourage the sharing of ideas, knowledge, and interaction with those of similar interests. The

ABOVE **Denis Shaw (U.S.A.)** brings to his designs his concerns for environmental issues. "Ursus," made in 1991, captures all the grace and ferocity of wild animals.

LEFT **"Antique Gray Bear"** was made by **Barbara Conley (U.S.A.)** in 1993 using traditional style and methods (height 15½ inches).

RIGHT **Dee Hockenberry, (U.S.A.)** creator of **"Mr. Bruin"** (1990, height 13 inches), is one of the world's leading authorities on old bears in addition to being a talented artist.

ABOVE **Betsy Reum's (U.S.A.)** "Puppeteer" was made in 1987 as part of a limited edition of 100 bears. She produces exciting and varied designs that are highly collectible.

ABOVE **"Buster" by Brian Beacock (Britain)** was made in 1987 and measures 20 inches. Dr. Brian is probably better known as a teddy bear restorer, but he has designed several bears for production.

RIGHT **"Hans-Werner Jager"** was made by the German artist Heike Gumpp (height 20½ inches). "The Hunter" illustrates Heike's wonderful eye for detail.

ABOVE **"Big Friendly Guy"** was made by Jo Greeno one of Britain's best artists, especially for the author's store.

LEFT **"Ebenezer"** was created by New Zealanders Michael and Judy Walton in 1993 (height 20 inches). Artists in the southern hemisphere are beginning to receive the recognition they deserve.

ABOVE **"Gerry's Teddy at Play" was
created especially for the authors by Jane
Humme of the Netherlands in 1993
(height 3½ inches).**

movement grew rapidly, resulting in the production of
new and exciting teddy bears at a time when collectors
were really hungry for something different, individual,
and not too expensive. There was an immediate rapport
with collectors which has grown and lasted to this day.
Subsequently, the influence of the America bear artist
spread to other countries, in particular to Britain, while
the Netherlands, Germany, Australia, New Zealand,
and Japan are now beginning to develop their own artist
bear markets.

American artists have given the lead which other
new artists around the world should appreciate and,
while still developing their own ideas, gladly follow. In
Britain, the standard of artist teddy bears has improved
enormously to the point where the creations of some
potentially excellent artists are often equal to those
produced by American artists; and this is now
beginning to happen in other countries, too.

Without doubt, the artist bear is currently the vogue,
and an enormous international market has developed
which is presently the most important of the three
genres (old, contemporary, and artists) covered in this
book. This happened partly because of the high prices
demanded for old bears, and partly because
contemporary alternatives were becoming predictable
and relatively far too expensive.

The tremendous variety, individuality, and quality
provided by artist bears probably satisfies the needs of
many present-day collectors, who are more
sophisticated, well-informed, discerning, and
demanding than those a decade ago.

ABOVE **This appealing bear
called "Marvin" was made by
Austrian artist Karin
Kronsteiner in 1993 (height
27½ inches).**

BELOW **"Marvin the Magician"
was made in 1993 by one of
Britain's top artists – Naomi
Laight. She rarely dresses her
bears, but Marvin shows her
skillful use of antique
materials.**

Artists everywhere now produce store-specials, limited editions, one-of-a-kind bears, as well as charitable donations and show pieces. There is a tremendously exciting variety of bears available to collectors to suit all tastes and pockets. One of the most appealing factors, however, is that the vast majority of artists simply abhor the idea of producing large numbers of the same bear. The restricted production does, of course, greatly enhance future investment prospects; the one-of-a-kind bears and small-quantity editions are likely to be the rarities for future generations of collectors. Of course, anyone can make a single bear, but it is the special edition teddy bears produced by distinguished artists that are likely to prove the best investment prospects.

However, no one can ever be quite sure precisely what future generations of arctophiles will prefer, so why not just enjoy collecting artist bears regardless of their potential value?

ABOVE **British artist Maddie Jones made "Algie" with hand-dyed mohair. He was made in 1993 and measures 18 inches.**

LEFT **There is precision and quality in Nancy Crowe's (U.S.A.) work. "Sandman" was made in 1993 and measures 15 inches.**

RIGHT **"Amelia Earheart" is one of Betsy Reum's (U.S.A.) most popular designs. She measures 10 inches and was made in 1993.**

BELOW **Rosalie Frischmann's (U.S.A.) bears are highly sought. "Murphy" was made in 1991 and measures 23 inches.**

ABOVE **Gregory Gyllenship is one of a handful of British male teddy bear artists. He prefers traditional designs, as can be seen from "Alexander" (seated) and "Gilbert." (Height 16 inches, 1993.)**

RIGHT **Janet Clark's (U.K.) captivating bear and bunnie called "Sophie" was made for the Teddies of the World '93 convention. (Height 22 inches).**

ABOVE **More appealing creations from Dee Hockenberry (U.S.A.). These are called "Timeless Teddies" and measure 12 inches and 14 inches. They were made in 1993.**

RIGHT **"Debbie" is a teenager from the 1950s and a big Elvis fan, of course! She was made by Diane Gard (U.S.A.) in 1994 in a limited edition of ten and measures 30 inches.**

ABOVE **Lynda Graves (U.K.) prefers to make very small numbers of her character bears. "Stargazer" was made in 1993 in a limited edition of three. (Height 16 inches).**

ABOVE **Celia Baham (U.S.A.) is a prolific and very creative artist. The "Roosevelt Bear" shown is from her second edition. He was made in 1993 and measures 18 inches.**

ABOVE **Sue Quinn's popularity has spread from her native Britain to the rest of the world. "Sugar Plum Bear" was made in 1993 and measures 13 inches.**

ABOVE **Billee Henderson (U.S.A.) is an award-winning bear designer who can turn her hand to a variety of styles. "James," a traditional bear, was made in 1993.**

ABOVE **These delightful clown bears named "Cornetto" and "Pauro" were made by Shirley Latimer (U.K.) in 1993. They measure 15 and 7½ inches.**

ABOVE **Before turning her talents to artist bears, Pam Howells (U.K.) was a designer for Chiltern. "Charlotte" was made in 1993 and measures 23 inches.**

ABOVE **American Ena Hammond creates bears with distinctive personalities. Ena made "Wooly Bear" in 1991. He measures 12 inches.**

ABOVE **Teresa Rowe is one of Britain's up and coming artists. The "Mad Hatter," a character from *Alice in Wonderland*, was made in 1994 and measures 12 inches.**

ABOVE **Kathy Wallace (U.S.A.) has been making bears since 1982. Her designs are traditional and full of character. "German Gold" measures 24½ inches (1991).**

ABOVE **Anne Inman (U.S.A.) is renowned for her innovative ideas. "Strawberries and Cream" is filled with perfumed pellets! She was made in 1993 (height 19 inches).**

ABOVE **Composition pieces are always in demand. "The Strawberry Picker" by Linda Edwards (U.K.) is a stunning creation made in 1993 measuring 17 inches.**

ABOVE **These traditionally dressed bears, "Sumo bear Yokozuna" and "Kimono," were created by Japanese artist Terumi Nishiyama in 1993. (Height 5 inches.)**

LEFT **"Huxley" by Denis Shaw (U.S.A.), is an appealing interpretation of a real bear. He was made in 1993 and measures 9½ inches.**

RIGHT **"Emmett" is part of Steve Schutt's wonderful Bedy-By series. The long-limbed design is very distinctive. He was made in 1991 (height 14½ inches).**

ABOVE **"Fleur" and "Ice Crystal" were made by up and coming miniaturist, Britain's Louise Peers. Made in 1993, they measure 3 inches.**

ABOVE **The quality and detail of this delightful bear by Marcia Sibol (U.S.A.) speaks for itself. "Jenny" was made in 1991 and measures 14½ inches.**

ABOVE **"Mother and Baby" 2⅞/6 inches by Grandma Lynn Lumley (U.S.A.) c. 1993. This Toby Award winning artist specializes in bears between 4 and 7 inches, uniquely costumed.**

ABOVE **One of America's most successful artists, Janet Reeves' makes bears in demand worldwide. "Miss Hildegard" was made in 1993 and measures 17½ inches.**

ABOVE **Mary Holden (U.K.) likes to keep her bears as environmentally friendly as possible by using natural wool fillings. "Baby George" measures 18 inches (1994).**

ABOVE **Michi Takahashi's (Japan) bears are always fun and these "Fairy Chuckles" are no exception. They were made in 1993 and measure 2¾ inches and 6 inches.**

LEFT **"Luke" is another example of the delightful, characterful bears being created by the talented Dutch artist Jane Humme. (Height 18 cm/7 in, 1993.)**

RIGHT **"The Applepicker" was made by Teresa Brookes and Barbara Percival, who incidentally are sisters. This bear, made in 1994, measures 12 inches.**

ABOVE **"Pearly King and Queen" were made by Nicola Perkins (U.K.), a top miniaturist. These two traditional British characters measure 3 inches.**

ABOVE **Barbara Ferrier (USA) produces bears in an enormous variety of styles. "Panda" is an unusual miniature bear made in 1991 and measuring 10 cm/4 in.**

ABOVE **"Blue Bear" is one of American Brenda Dewey's popular fantasy bears. It was made in 1993 and measures 5 inches.**

WHERE AND HOW TO BUY

CHAPTER 6

The problems facing every collector are what to collect and how much to spend. You have to decide whether collecting is purely to satisfy a love of bears, or whether it is a matter of investment. Both have quite different requirements. There are a whole host of possible sources of where to buy or sell teddy bears, all of which have advantages and, dare we say, pitfalls.

RARITY FACTOR

However popular they all may appear, it is obvious that some teddy bears are rarer than others, usually because very few were ever made. Sometimes rarity is assumed because it may be extremely difficult to attribute a bear of undoubted quality and appeal to a specific manufacturer. Fortunately, some manufacturers are well-known, and particular items can be positively identified from company records and other reliable sources; Steiff is a prime example, but even then positive substantiation is sometimes difficult. All too often reliable information about a manufacturer is scarce or even nonexistent. This fact creates an awful dilemma for those with the responsibility of trying to determine authenticity.

LEFT *The Teddy Bear Shop* is an original painting by teddy bear lover and artist Diane Elson (1988).

ABOVE This musical bear was originally attributed to Schuco. We think it is more likely to be by Eduard Cramer.

The question of rarity is of little relevance if the particular teddy bear is so unattractive or crudely made that no one could possibly be interested. The law of supply and demand really determines the value of most bears, whether rare or not! Many contemporary manufactured limited editions become scarce after only a few years, and is not the artist "one-of-a-kind" creation potentially a rare piece?

ABOVE **A one-of-a-kind bear that is potentially very valuable: "Old Time American** **Policeman" made by Betsy Reum (U.S.A.) in 1993 and measuring 16 inches.**

ABOVE **This 3½-inch bear was sold as a 1930s Steiff teddy baby. It is in fact from the** **1950s. Teddy babies from this era are much harder to find and so are more valuable!**

PROVENANCES

As we have mentioned frequently in this book, establishing the age of a particular bear is very difficult and should never be considered a precise science – except when indisputable evidence exists, it is often a matter of judgment based on experience.

Frequently, people spurred on by the prospect that the bear may be worth a lot of money foolishly assume that granny's bear must be about her age! A lady once tried to tell us that her bear had to be 110 years old because her grandmother (dead then, of course) had been born around 1885. She could not believe us when we said no teddy bear could be that old. She might not have known that, but she didn't even realize that *nylon* teddies were not made until the 1950s! Many people seem convinced that they know exactly their bear's age and do not like being contradicted. Irrefutable evidence, however, can be provided by a picture of a child with a bear, preferably dated, together with other supporting written documentation.

Of course, we all know of many people, often in the trade, who sadly have remarkably fertile and imaginative ideas about a bear's age and history when it comes to selling! It is always difficult to be sure any information is accurate, so be cautious.

ABOVE **This style of bear has often been attributed to J. K. Farnell, but this unusual white** **bear from the late 1930s is unmistakably a Chiltern.**

FAKES

It is sad to reflect that with greater public awareness of the potential value of an old teddy, unscrupulous people have now taken to faking bears. If you accept that manufacturers make pretty good copies of their old bears, and that some artists are capable of producing really good old-looking bears, then you realize how easy it is to mislead the inexperienced collector. Faking can therefore be a very lucrative pastime for crooks!

Most people involved in faking bears are fairly unsophisticated, so they frequently let themselves down, though occasionally you might come up against a good forgery, so be careful – and remember it is not necessarily the most expensive bear that can provide the forger with a good living! If you have the slightest doubt or suspicion, leave the bear well alone!

HOW TO SPOT A FAKE

▌ Rub your hands fairly lightly over the bear's fur – if your hands soil easily, it is likely that the grime was recently applied.

▌ Smell the bear – it should have a natural, old, fusty smell and not a distinct odor of tobacco or dirt.

▌ Look at the wear and tear. Cuts and tears are rarely a precise clean cut such as one made by a knife. Mohair wear is naturally intermittent and uneven. Therefore, look closely at the backing of the pile and any fine line marks caused by wire brush or sandpaper, frequently used to enhance wear, will be obvious. A disk or brush applied with an electric drill will leave a distinct circular pattern.

▌ However well kept, most bears 40 or more years old inevitably have suffered discoloration of some form or other. Look in the joints and you will see the bear's natural color but expect some deterioration elsewhere. The fur of a recently made bear looks fairly consistent all over.

▌ Finally, just hold the bear, because modern filled bears look and feel distinctively different from old ones, although you will need some experience to recognize this.

RIGHT **This unusual two-tone bear was made by Chad Valley in the 1930s. Although there is some wear, it would be a great find for a collector.**

BELOW **The button is missing, but the quality and design tell you this bear was made by Steiff (1907/08). It is less risky to buy bears like this from reputable dealers.**

ATTRIBUTES TO LOOK FOR IN AN OLD BEAR

If your reason for buying is just because you love looking after old bears, then probably all you will need to do is make eye contact (with the bear, not the seller), and if you are not immediately attracted, then you probably never will be!

First, character, which is a very subjective matter, is probably the essential factor. Condition will also be an important consideration in old bears. It is a matter of personal preference as to what you are prepared to accept. Do not expect bears to be in pristine condition; indeed, well-loved bears are frequently far better characters when they have been played with.

SPECIALIST COLLECTORS' STORES

In the U.S., Britain, and the Netherlands, specialist collectors' shops are plentiful, and they are now beginning to spring up in other countries, too. It is necessary to define what a specialist collectors' shop constitutes. In our view it is a shop that caters exclusively to the collector and not the tourist or off-the-street trade, and certainly not a gift, antique, or general toy store. While many of the latter may be perfectly reliable, they cannot ever be considered in the same category as the specialist shop which has dedicated itself totally to serving collectors. Some specialist shops deal only in old bears, while others sell contemporary and artist collectibles, and some deal in all three categories.

Collectors will soon discover which shops to patronize, and those which can be entirely relied upon for their professional, ethical approach and standards. As with all collectibles, there are specialists who have been established much longer than others, and are highly regarded with a reputation gained over the years for fair dealing. In general, these dealers are also capable of providing a reliable advisory service including valuation and identification.

CHECK POINTS FOR CONDITION

Compare the color of mohair in the joints with the rest of the bear as you can determine just how faded the bear actually is. It might be seriously faded, but perhaps it has just grown old gracefully just like a human. Mohair should generally be in satisfactory condition.

▌ The facial embroidering should match the general demeanor of the bear; if it is bright and fresh, it was probably added recently. This would not perhaps matter too much, but often the wrong style of nose or mouth is sewn, giving the bear quite a false look. Of course, this could have happened 40 years before on a visit to a teddy bear hospital, which is why you need to know as much as possible about the original style of nose.

▌ Are the eyes original? There is a very good chance they they are not! If not, make sure they are the right size and color and have been fitted properly.

▌ Are the limbs well retained or have some discreetly hidden stitches been added to anchor the head or legs?

▌ Are there any tears in the fabric, split seams, or damaged pads?

▌ Does the voice box or squeaker work? Most of them do not, and sadly, the modern day replacement is often poor in comparison and distinctly noticeable.

LEFT **There are many teddy bear shops which sell only artist bears like "Buster" by Rosalie Frischmann (U.S.A.) and "Carmel" by Joan Woessner (U.S.A.).**

RIGHT **Another modern collectible – the first in Steiff's British Collectors series (1989).**

SPECIALIST COLLECTORS' FAIRS/SHOWS

Teddy bear fairs are springing up everywhere, and in general the leading fairs are definitely going to be your best opportunity to seek out both old and new bears. Nowhere else will there be such quantity of delectable teddy bears, because the top events usually attract the nation's best specialist shops, dealers, and of course artists. At these fairs, you will also meet some independent dealers who do not have stores, but many of whom will have a good selection of bears for sale. Other participants at these shows are the artists and bear-makers, providing a splendid opportunity to purchase examples of their wonderful bears directly and also to learn more about their craft.

ABOVE **This is "Munchie," a one-off creation by Steve Schutt (height 36 inches). One of the great things about teddy** bear conventions is that top artists often create special one-off bears for the auctions and competitions.

There are now a veritable host of well-established teddy bear fairs in the U.S., Britain, and elsewhere. Many are well-organized and well worth attending. In addition, there is a plethora of smaller events which could be worth visiting, too; there is always the possibility that you will find something unexpected and interesting, particularly from a less experienced dealer.

ANTIQUE FAIRS/SHOWS

At the average antique collectors' fair, you are lucky to find more than one or two dealers selling teddy bears. Usually, though not always, there are a few old bears to be found among the general dealers, but these are often poor quality, over-priced, and frequently inappropriately and ambitiously identified.

We offer a serious word of caution because, although only occasionally, it is probably at antique fairs that you are most likely to encounter a fake or even a stolen teddy bear. The gullibility of some people when confronted by a "bargain" teddy being sold by a dealer who quite clearly would sell his own granny never ceases to amaze us.

Be warned and *be careful*, and do not buy anything you cannot be positive about.

TEDDY BEAR CONVENTIONS

American society was raised on conventions, and it is therefore inevitable that these would be organized from the time there were enough teddy bear fanatics to attend. Although the small convention has largely given way to the likes of Disney (doll and teddy bear combined), they all remain very good opportunities for collectors, particularly because their favorite artists or manufacturers are present to sign their bears or generally just talk.

Conventions are now beginning in other parts of the world. Teddies of the World '93 held in Northampton, England, was exclusively concerned with teddy bears old and new and was the first of its kind, with an emphasis on all facets of collecting. Japan has recently held its first collectors' convention.

At all of these events, artists are usually invited to produce special one-of-a-kind bears for auction. Frequently, all the proceeds are given to charity, but this is not always the case. This provides yet another excellent opportunity to obtain that really special example of an artist's work.

AUCTION HOUSES

The U.S. and Britain probably have the finest auction houses in the world, all holding regular sales. Usually, they are combined toy, doll, and teddy bear auctions where you can buy or arrange to sell, but you will have to pay a premium of between 10 and 15 percent for the service. If you want an independent assessment of potential value, auction houses are an obvious and generally accepted source.

Auction houses unquestionably have the advantage of being able to reach a much larger market because their client base includes both trade buyers and private collectors. Consequently, they are more likely to achieve prices which possibly concur with your own expectations, should you wish to sell.

One word of caution though – over the past few years television programs dealing with antiques in general have shown bias in perpetuating the idea that auction houses are the only places for buying and selling. It is perfectly true they have produced some fabulously high sale prices, but these are definitely the exception rather than the rule. When it comes to identification, the leading specialists are generally equal if not better.

ABOVE **It is easy to identify this Merrythought bear because of its condition and label. This is** **not always the case, and specialist advice is advisable before selling.**

ANTIQUE STORES

These are always worth exploring because even if you do not find any bears, you might still find some splendid teddy memorabilia or a delightful old costume for your favorite bear.

The obvious problem with antique stores is that because they have to deal with a wide range of artifacts, they generally lack specialist knowledge about bears. They also often depend on general antique pricing guides, and you may well find any bears optimistically priced, to put it mildly.

ABOVE **When it comes to positively identifying your teddy bears, leading specialists are just as reliable as the** **auction houses. Left to right: 1950s Merrythought, Schuco "Yes-No" from c. 1935 and a 1920s Gebrüder Bing.**

GARAGE SALES

We constantly get asked about the value of bears which were found at these sales. Nine hundred and ninety-nine times out of a thousand, the bear is probably not of any real value, but very occasionally someone has had a really good find. There is always a chance of this, but in our experience, you had better be prepared to spend many long and fruitless hours searching.

These sales can, however, be a good source for those of you who are not all concerned with the value but just want to give a new home to a poor discarded teddy. You are more likely to find teddies from the 1970s and 1980s who are in need of a more appreciative new guardian.

MAGAZINES

Teddy bear magazines often carry "For sale" advertisements, and these can be useful. However, you often have to buy sight unseen, and your interpretation

ABOVE **It is still possible to find cheap, unidentified old bears. From studying this bear, our guess would be that it was made by the British World War I manufacturer W. H. Jones.**

of "pristine" is likely to be quite different from the seller's; nor can you always be sure that it is a genuine private sale. You take a chance always whether you are buying or selling.

WHEN BUYING AND SELLING . . .

DO	DON'T
▌ Try to find out as much as you can about the bear; family photographs and other provenances are a definite advantage.	▌ Do not believe everything you are told, particularly when looking at old bears!
▌ Buy from reliable people.	▌ When selling, do not hand over the bear to a would-be purchaser without full payment unless he or she is a reputable dealer.
▌ Make sure the choice is definitely yours and not a persuasive salesperson's technique.	▌ Do not buy from anyone you feel you cannot trust.
▌ Take account of the extra commission or premiums you will have to pay if buying or selling at auction.	▌ Do not buy unless you are absolutely sure this is the bear you really want.
▌ Thoroughly check the bear before purchasing to make sure it is in good condition and is what it is supposed to be. (Sometimes, of course, the bear has been attributed to the wrong maker, which might just occasionally benefit you.)	▌ Do not buy for investment only; this will prevent you from being upset if the teddy bear's value does not increase as quickly as you would wish.
	▌ Do not buy limited editions without their certificate or box.
	▌ Do not buy inferior quality unless of course you want to. Contemporary bears which are damaged in any way should be totally avoided.

CARE AND REPAIRS

All bears benefit from being properly looked after, and the following advice may be of some guidance.

What should I do when I bring home a newly purchased bear?

You might be surprised by what can be found inside old bears. This warm and safe habitat is a delightful haven for all types of bugs and parasites, which can easily spread to the rest of your collection if you are not careful. One solution which seems to offer some, though not complete, protection is to wrap any newly purchased bear in a plastic bag and leave it in the freezer for at least 48 hours. As an extra protection, you might consider adding some flea powder (vacuum off afterward).

Some people use moth balls, but we do not advocate this method because of the smell. We discovered an old English 19th-century recipe from *Mrs Beeton's Household Management*, which advocates sprinkling whole cloves in small dishes and placing them among your bears. The smell is not strong to humans, and it seems to work. Another solution is to buy impregnated wooden cedar blocks, as most insects do not appear to like them.

We have been asked if bears can be protected from bugs by putting them inside glass cabinets. Bugs will usually get in despite this precaution, but it will of course help to keep the bears clean.

Remember, you constantly need to inspect your teddies and clean them.

LEFT Jo Greeno's "Miss Marple" and Gary Nett's (U.S.A.) "Father Christmas" investigate the mysterious death of a 1905 center seam Steiff!

RIGHT With a little care and attention, this Steiff bear from the 1920s can be brought back to pristine condition.

How should I clean my bears?

Mohair, alpaca, and wool are the main materials used for making old bears; being natural fibers, these are all washable. However, never immerse a teddy in water – it would have a devastating effect; wash the surface of your bears only.

Use a mild detergent mixed with warm water and whipped to produce a foam (test first that this does not make the material fade). Using a soft cloth or a soft baby's brush, rub or stipple this into the mohair. Do not use a stiff or hard bristle or nylon brush as it might damage the backing of the fabric or pull out the fibers. Stubborn stains can be removed by the use of a bristle toothbrush (soft to medium), but be careful.

When you are satisfied (you can soon tell as your bowl of water should be discolored), remove the suds with a clean wet cloth. After the suds have been removed, go over the bear again with warm water to which a little fabric conditioner has been added, and rub this all over the bear. Afterward, rub the surface carefully with a clean towel to remove excess moisture.

A hairdryer set to low heat is a very useful way of quick drying, but remember how you dry your own hair, and using the same technique (no rollers please!), continually brush the fabric if you wish to "style" or control the lay of the pile. When the bear is dry, we always place it in a warm, dark cupboard for 48 hours because this will dry out the bear slowly and thoroughly.

It is often very difficult to clean a teddy bear made of synthetic materials, although you can try the same method as given above. However, these bears were often manufactured to enable them to be totally immersed in water so you may therefore be able to wash them by hand (check the label). Remember, teddy would not like to take a trip in your washing machine or tumble dryer!

How should I regularly clean my bears other than by surface wash?

Inspect your bears regularly for infestation, dust, and so on, and keep the fur clean by vacuuming them. Be careful that you do not apply excessive suction – it will be all too easy to skin a bear or remove a loose eye or that valuable name tag or label. Guard against this by covering the vacuum nozzle with a nylon stocking.

LEFT **This large (26-inch) 1930s Chad Valley is potentially valuable and would benefit from professional restoration of the foot pads.**

RIGHT **These 1930s bears are made of art silk plush which, unlike mohair, does not clean easily.**

If I really cannot bring myself to subject my teddy to surgery, what other practical hints can you advise?

Damaged hand and foot pads can be temporarily protected by using babies' gloves and booties. Frail bodies, arms, and legs can also be protected by dressing teddy in an old one-piece baby suit, or simply sweater and pants.

Do bears and live animals go well together?

No, because it is well known that dogs and cats can carry all sorts of fleas and other bugs, which might just be looking for a new habitat! Also, no teddy would enjoy being picked up and shaken in a dog's mouth, or clawed by a cat, any more than you would.

Will smoking have any effect on my bears?

Bears are affected by passive smoking just as humans are because the smell lingers in their fur – but it's really up to you. We do not allow anyone to smoke in our store or in our home, and that way our teddies smell fragrant.

I am worried about insuring my collection. What should I do?

You should definitely get your bears cataloged and properly insured. This is not as expensive as you might think, and even though much of your collection might be irreplacable, at least adequate insurance will be some recompense should something happen. We recommend that you also get an effective security alarm system installed, including fire detection, as this will almost certainly be in your favor when arranging for insurance and, of course, give you peace of mind.

Make a careful list with as much information as possible about your bears – date of purchase, how much they cost, size, make, and so on. It may also be necessary to obtain an independent valuation by a teddy bear specialist, but this probably depends on how valuable your collection is and how comprehensive your records are. Photographing all your bears is another good idea, but it is much easier, quicker, and cheaper to video them. Remember to make duplicate copies and deposit them in the bank or some other safe place, not in your house in case it was ever seriously damaged.

LEFT **It is probably too late to do much more than a careful surface wash on this 1938 Merrythought Dutch boy.**

RIGHT **This 1930 Chad Valley has also suffered the ravages of time, and it is best just to give it a surface wash.**

What if my bear needs repairing?

If your bear is in need of major repair or restoration or if it is very valuable, then we would recommend the services of a reputable bear repairer or hospital. Check the credentials of the repairers first and ask to see some of their work, or better still ask to speak to someone who has used the repairer before. We would *never* advocate your attempting major repair yourself unless you are experienced!

If your bear needs a minor repair, you may feel competent enough to tackle this yourself. A split seam or loose pad can easily be repaired, provided you are competent with a needle and thread. Should you need to darn a nose, mouth or paw, make sure you use the same color floss. *Never* change the pattern of these features – always copy exactly the method of application used by the manufacturer. This is not as easy as it looks, and you can totally destroy the character of your bear.

Eyes should only be replaced if one is broken or missing. Here again, you must try to match the original eye both in color and size. To make sure teddy has the right eyes, pads or facial features, thoroughly research in this and the many other authoritative books that exist. Remember, many old bears have had their noses and eyes changed, so if the opportunity arises, make sure you replace them by the correct style or type of eye. Most eyes are sewn to the lower back of the head, but some were sewn through the ears. If in doubt, get the work carried out by a proper repairer.

Why has my teddy discolored over the past few years if he has only been kept in the living room?

No fabric, except some man-made fibers, tolerates direct exposure to sunlight. *Always keep bears away from direct or excessive sunlight*. In fact, keep the curtains closed as much as possible to reduce the amount of light in the room. Lace curtains will also help to cut down light penetration. Move your teddies around the room constantly so that none of them get more sunlight than is good for them. Unlike humans, a teddy bear will not get a tan if left in the sun, but more likely a most unhealthy pale complexion (due to discoloration)!

LEFT **This 1960s Chiltern Hugmee looks much better after a wash and brush up.**

RIGHT **A 1930s Merrythought that has been partially bleached by strong light.**

LEARNING MORE ABOUT BEARS

CHAPTER 8

In order to derive the maximum benefit from collecting teddy bears, you owe it to yourself, and your bank account, to obtain as much knowledge as is possible. The more proficient you are at identifying old bears, recognizing a good bargain, or appreciating investment potential (this applies to both new and old bears), the less likely you are to make a serious – and therefore costly – mistake. The following sources may help to improve your knowledge.

MUSEUMS

Although there are a great many toy museums, we frequently find those which claim to have "many teddy bears" rarely do and are thus rather disappointing. This is particularly true of those in Germany. We would, however, suggest that whenever possible, you should try to make a visit because even if a museum contains only a few examples, these can all enhance your appreciation of teddy bears. These are just a few museums you should *not* miss:

U.S.A.
The Teddy Bear Museum of Naples, Florida

BRITAIN
The Cotswold Teddy Bear Museum, High Street, Broadway, Worcestershire WR12 7AJ
The Bear Museum, 38 Dragon Street, Petersfield, Hampshire GU31 4JJ

GERMANY
Margarete Steiff Museum, Allen Strasse 2, D-7928 Giengen (Brenz)

RIGHT **Examine your bears thoroughly – this 1930s Chad Valley had a button attached to the back of the shoulder adding to its value.**

LEFT **Gary Nett's "Mr. Cinammon" bear is in a studious mood. He was made in 1983 and measures 18 inches.**

SHOWS AND CONVENTIONS

These can be both tremendous fun and beneficial in providing opportunities to add to your collection and share joyful experiences with other collectors.

There are a considerable number of events in the USA and Europe but only the very best shows and conventions attract the big names in the teddy bear world.

USA

ABC Unlimited Promotions Shows, Schaumberg, Illinois, and other locations *(several)*

Bill Boyd's Teddy Bear Jubilee, Kansas City, Missouri *(annual)*

Serena Cohen's, Libearty Weekend Artist Bear Show, Philadelphia, Pennsylvania *(annual)*

Disneyland Doll and Bear Convention, Anaheim, California *(annual)*

Disney World Doll and Bear Conventions, Florida *(annual)*

Donna Harrison's Shows and Convention, Baltimore, Maryland *(twice yearly)*

ILTBC Convention, Orange, California *(annual)*

Linda Mullins Shows, San Diego, California *(twice yearly)*

Steve Schutt's, Teddy Bear Reunion in the Heartland, Clarion, Iowa *(every five years, next in June 1995)*

JAPAN

Japan Teddy Bear Association Convention, Tokyo *(annual)*

UK

Margaret and Gerry Grey's Teddies of the World Convention, location to be confirmed *(every three years, next in 1996)*

Hugglets, Teddy Bear Fairs and events, London and Stratford-on-Avon *(several)*

Teddy Bear Times, British Bear Festivals, Croydon, and Hove, East Sussex *(twice yearly)*

THE NETHERLANDS

Rob and Inge Kuiters, Bear Festival Amerongen Castle *(every May)*

MAGAZINES

There are many very good specialist magazines published throughout the world which you will find an extremely valuable source of information.

Bear Facts Review, published in Australia

Beer Bericht, published in the Netherlands (four issues)

Ciesliks Teddy und seine Freunde, published in Germany

de Teddy-Beer, published in the Netherlands (four issues)

Hugglets Teddy Bear Magazine, published in UK (four issues)

Teddy Bear and Friends, published in USA (six issues)

Teddy Bear Review, published in USA (five issues)

Teddy Bear Times, published in UK (six issues)

RECOMMENDED READING

There are many wonderful books, all of which we unfortunately cannot list here. Every single teddy bear book you can lay your hands on should be read because with each one there is always something new to learn and improve your knowledge. Particular books we would positively recommend as very useful and entertaining are the following:

Peter Bull, *Teddy Bear Book* (1969)

Jurgen and Marianne Cieslik, *Button in the Ear* (1989)

Hobby House Teddy Bear & Friends Price Guides – Nos. 1, 2, 3 and 4 (1993)

Pauline Cockrill, *The Ultimate Teddy Bear Book* (1991), and *The Teddy Bear Encyclopedia* (1993)

Dee Hockenberry, *Collectible German Animals Value Guide 1948 to 1968* (1989), and *Bear Memorabilia* (1992)

Margaret Hutchings, *The Book of the Teddy Bear* (1964)

Ted Menten, *Teddy's Bearzaar* (1988), and *Teddy Bear Lovers Companion* (1989)

Linda Mullins, *Teddy Bears Past and Present*, Vol I (1986) and Vol II (1991)

Romy Roeder, *Teddy Bears, Golliwogs and Playmates of the Past* (1988)

Patricia N. Schoonmaker, *A Collector's History of the Teddy Bear* (1981)

Rosemary and Paul Volpp, *A Beary Merry Christmas* (1987), and *A Bear for all Seasons* (1989)

Carol-Lynn Rössell Waugh, *Teddy Bear Artists – Romance of Making and Collecting Bears* (1984)

CLUBS AND ASSOCIATIONS

These are obviously worth considering because you will be able to meet people with similar interests. There are now a vast number of collectors' clubs; some associated with manufacturers such as the Steiff Club, some with magazines such as the *Teddy Bear Times* British Bear Club, the International League of Teddy Bear Clubs in the USA, and those with solely charitable intentions such as Good Bears of the World – covering just about every conceivable facet of collecting.

Our personal preference is however, for the less formal type of small local self-run clubs such as the one we belong to called the Bear Talk Club, in Stratford-on-Avon, UK.

Details of clubs and associations are listed regularly in leading collectors' magazines.

INDEX

A

Acton Toy Craft Ltd 34
Aerolite 20, *20*, 22
Aetna 13
"Still Hope" *11*
Ahsolight 20
American Doll and Toy
  Manufacturing Co 14
antique stores and fairs 70, 71
Applause 41
Atlas Manufacturing Co 15
auctions 71
Australian bears
  interwar 28–9
  postwar 37–9
Austrian bears 39

B

Baham, Celia
  "Roosevelt Bear" *62*
Baxter, Thomas 16
Beacock, Brian
  "Buster" *58*
Bearly There Inc 41
Berg 39
Berg, Herman 10
Berlex Toy Pty 28, 37, *37*
Berryman, Clifford 9, 10
Bing, Gebrüder (later Bing-
  Werke) 12, *12*, *17*, 26, *26*
Bingie bear 24, *24*
Blackburn, John and Maude 41
  "Rosie" *41*
books, teddy bear 78
Borgfeldt, Geo 10, 14
Boston, Wendy
  Playsafe bears 32, *32*
British bears
  early distributors 16–17
  early manufacture 12, 15–16
  interwar years 19, 21–5
  limited editions 41–3
  postwar years 32–5
  teddy bear artists 59
British United Toy
  Manufacturing Co 16
Brookes, Teresa and Percival,
  Barbara
  "The Applepicker" *65*
Bruin Manufacturing 13
Bull, Peter 6, 8, 42, 55
Butler Bros 14
buying bears 66–72

C

Calvin, Karin and Howard *57*
Canham, Deborah
  circus bears *54*
Canterbury Bears 41, *41*, 42
Chad Valley
  Aerolite 20, *20*, 22
  dating 22
  interwar bears *7*, 20, *20*,
    21–3, *22*
  Magna 22
  Peacock 22, *22*, 23
  postwar bears 30, *30*, 32, *32*
Character Novelty Co 31, *31*

Chiltern bears
  Baby Bruin 34
  Cubby 25
  early bears 15–16
  Hugmee 24, *25*, 34, *34*, *76*
  interwar 20, 24–5
  Master Teddy 1915 *15*
  postwar 34
  Silky Teddy 20
  Skater Bear *25*
  Ting-a-Ling Bear 34
Clark, Janet
  "Loving" *55*
  "Sophie" *61*
cleaning bears 73–5
clubs and associations 78
Columbia Teddy Bear
  Manufacturing 14
  Laughing Roosevelt Bear *14*
Commonwealth Toy and Novelty
  Co
  "Feed me" bear 21
condition of bears 68–9
Conley, Barbara *8*
  "Antique Gray Bear" *57*
conventions 70
Cramer, Eduard 28
Cranshaw, Anne *57*
  "Casco Bear" *57*
Cray and Nicholls 16
Crowe, Nancy
  "Sandman" *60*

D

dating bears 22, 67
Deans Rag Book Co Ltd
  collectibles 42
  earliest bears 15
  interwar 23, *23*
  postwar 33, *33*
Dehler, E. 18
Dewey, Brenda
  "Wizard" *54*, "Blue Bear" *65*
Dreamland Doll Company 14

E

East London Toy Factory
  (EALON) 16, 25
Edwards, Linda
  "The Strawberry Picker" *64*
Eisemann, Josef 16
ELI 18
Emil Toys 28, *29*, 38, *38*
Epstein, B. 14

F

FADAP 29
fairs, specialist 70
fakes 68
Farnell, J. K.
  Alpha 23
  early bears 12, 15
  interwar *7*, *19*, 20, 23, *23*
  postwar 33, *33*
  Silkalite 20
Fast Black Shirt Co 14
Ferrier, Barbara
  "Panda" *65*
French bears 29

Frischmann, Rosalie
  "Buster" *69*
  "Murphy" *60*

G

Gard, Diane
  "Billy Ray" 55, *57*
  "Marisa Bearensen" *56*
  "Debbie" *61*
German bears
  early manufacturing 9,
    10–11, *12*, 17–18
  interwar years *19*, 21, 26–8
  limited editions 43–53
  postwar 35–37
Gillespie, Mrs G. C. 14
Gottschalk and Davis 16
Graves, Lynda
  "Stargazer" *62*
Greeno, Jo
  "Miss Marple" *54*, 73
  "Big Friendly Guy" *58*
Gumpp, Heike
  "Hans Werner Jager" *58*
Gund Manufacturing Co 14, 21,
  31
Gyllenship, Gregory
  "Alexander" and "Gilbert" *61*

H

Hammond, Ena
  "Woolly Bear" *63*
Harman Manufacturing Co 13
Harmus, Carl, Jr 18
Harwin and Company 15
  Ally Bears 15
Hecla Bear Co 13
Helvetic 29
Henderson, Billee
  "James" *62*
Hercules bears 17
Hermann, Gebrüder
  early bears 12, 18
  interwar 28
  postwar 35, *35*
  replicas 43, *43*
  Zotty 35
Hermann, Max (later Hermann-
  Spielwaren) 18, 27, 37
Hockenberry, Dee
  "Mr Bruin" *57*
  "Timeless Teddies" *61*
Hofmann, Carl 18
Holden, Mary
  "Baby George" *65*
Horsmann, E. C. and Co 14
Howells, Pam
  "Charlotte" *63*
Hughes, Herbert E. 16
Humme, Jane
  "Gerry's Teddy at Play" *59*
  "Luke" *65*
"Humpty Dumpty" toys 17
Hutchings, Margaret 55

I

Ideal Toy and Novelty Co 10, 13,
  13, 31
  "Charlamagne" *10*

Imperial Toy Co 16
Inman, Anne
  "Strawberries and Cream" *63*
insects, protection from 73
Institute of Hygiene mark of
  approval 20
insurance 75
Invicta Toys 25
Isaacs (ISA) 16, 22
Isenberg, Barbara 41

J

Jakas 38
Japanese bears 19, 30, *64*, *65*
Jones, Maddie
  "Algie" *60*
Jones, W. H. 17
Joy Toys Pty 29, *29*, 38, *38*
Jumbo Toys 17

K

Knickerbocker Toy Co Inc 19,
  21, *21*, 31, *31*
Kronsteiner, Karin
  "Marvin" *59*

L

Laight, Naomi
  "Marvin the Magician" *59*
Lakeland Bears *42*
Latimer, Shirley
  "Cornetto" and "Pauro" *62*
Leco Toys 34
Lefray Ltd 34, *35*
Leven, H. Josef, and Sprenger
  18, 28
Liebermann, Ernst, and Co 18
light, protecting from 76
Lindee Toys 39, *39*
Lines Brothers/International
  Model Aircraft Co Ltd *see*
  Pedigree
Little Folk 42
Lumley, Grandma Lynn
  "Mother and Baby" *64*

M

Madingland 17
magazines, 78
  buying from 72
Magna bears 22
Magnet bear 24
MAHESO 18, 28
Menten, Ted 56
  "Hug" 41, *41*
Merrythought Ltd 19, 24, 33
  Bingie 24, *24*
  Cheeky 33, *33*
  limited editions 42
  Magnet 24
  Punkinhead 33
Michtom, Morris and Rose 9–10
MICHU 18
Millas Manufacturing Co 14
Mutzi N. C. Z. 39

N

Nett, Gary and Margaret
  "Father Christmas" *54*

"Mr Cinnamon" 77
Nisbet, House of 42–3
  Bully Bear range 42
  Celebrity Collection 43, *43*
  Delicatessan 42, *42*
  Zodiac range 42
Nishiyama, Terumi
  "Sumo Bear Yokozuma" and
    "Kimono" *64*
North American Bear Co 41
  Hug 41, *41*
  Muffy 41
  V.I.P. range 41
  Vanderbear 41

O
Oppenheimer, S., Ltd 35

P
Peacock bears 22, *22*, 23
Pedigree 25, *25*, 33
Peers, Louise
  "Fleur" and "Ice Crystal" *64*
Perkins, Nicola
  "Pearly King and Queen" *65*
Petz Co 37
Pintel, M., Fils and Cie 29
Playsafe bears 32, *32*
Plummer and Wandless and Co
  Ltd 35
Port, Beverley 56

Q
Quinn, Sue
  "Sugar Plum Bear" *62*

R
Raikes, Robert, Originals 41
rarity 66–7
Rees, Leon, and Co *see* Chiltern
  Bears
Reeves, Janet
  "Miss Hildegard" *65*
repairing bears 76

replicas and special editions
  40–53
Reum, Betsy
  "Amelia Earheart" *60*
  "Old Time American
    Policeman" *67*
  "Puppeteer" *58*
Riley, Kathryn
  "Bearlin the White Wizard"
    55
Roosevelt, Theodore 9
Ross Toy Works 17
Rössel-Waugh, Carol-Lynn 56
  "Jenny-Lynn" *56*
Rouech-Bowden 14
Rowe, Teresa
  "Mad Hatter" *63*

S
Schuco (Schreyer and Co) 12,
  26, 36
  Bellhop bear 26
  Piccolo range 26, *26*
  Tricky 36
  tumbling bears 26
  Yes-No bear *20*, 21, 26, 35
Schutt, Steve 57
  "Emmett" *64*
  "Munchie" *70*
Shaw, Denis 57
  "Huxley" *64*
  "Ursus" *57*
shows and conventions 78
Sibol, Marcia
  "Jenny" *64*
  "Lady Margaret" *64*
silk plush bears, introduction of
  20
soft filled bears, introduction of
  10
"Softanlite" bears 17, 20
South Wales Toy Manufacturing
  Co 17
Steevans Musical Toys 17

Steiff, Margarete
  Barle range 10–11
  British Collection series *40*,
    52, 69
  button trademark 7, 11
  "Christian Gabriel" *10*
  Circus bears 27, 46
  "Dicky" 27, 46
  "Edelweiss" 7
  earliest bears 7, 10–11, *12*,
    18, *18*
  European Collectors Club 53
  "Happy" 21, *44*
  "Jackie" 37, *48*
  "King Arthur" *16*
  "Margaret Strong" 44, *44*
  interwar 20, 27, *27*
  limited editions 40, *40*,
    44–53
  model 5322 11
  PAB range 11, 18, *18*
  Petsy range 27, *27*, 50
  postwar 36, 37, *37*
  "Richard Steiff" *46*
  "Teddy Clown" 27, 46
  "Teddy Rose" *48*
  U.S. Collectors Club 53
  Zotty 7, *36*, 37
Steiff, Richard 9, 21
Stone, H. G. and Co Ltd *see*
  Chiltern
Stuffed Toy Co bears *12*
Süssenguth, Gebrüder
  Peter bear *20*, 28, *28*
Swiss bears 29, *39*

T
Tah Toys Ltd 25
Takahashi, Michi
  "Fairy Chuckles" *65*
Teddy Toy Company 17, 20, 25
  Softanlite 17, 20, 25
Terry, W. J. (Terryer Toys) 16,
  20

Thiennot 29
Tinka-Bell 35
Twyford bears 34

U
U.S. bears
  early distributors 14
  early manufacture 9–10,
    11–12, 13–14
  interwar years 19, 21
  limited editions 41
  postwar years 30, 31
  teddy bear artists 55–9
Uncle Remus Stuffed Toys 14

V
Verna 39, *39*
Very Important Bear (V.I.B.)
  range 41

W
W. T. Co 35
Wallace, Kathy
  "German Gold" *63*
Walton, Michael and Judy
  "Ebenezer" *58*
Whiteson Company 14
Wholesale Toy Company 17
Wilson, Jack 42
Woessner, Joan 57
  "Carmel" *69*
  "Elfinbeary Peach" *56*
Worthing Toy Factory 17
Wrekin Toy Company 17

Y
Yes-No bears *20*, 21, 26, 35
Young, A., and Son 17

Z
Zotty (Gebrüder Hermann) 35
Zotty (Steiff) 7, *36*, 37

ACKNOWLEDGMENTS

(Key: l = left, r = right, m = middle, be = below, t = top)

It would be impossible to write a book of this type without the assistance of others. We should particularly like to thank:

Des and Monica Carpenter, and son Mark, of The Cotswold Teddy Bear Museum, who allowed us to disrupt their splendid displays in order to photograph the lovely bears. (Bears on pages 7tl & bm, 15, 17br, 20tr & bl, 21, 22 bl & br, 23tl, tr & br, 24tl, tr & bl, 25bl, 26br, 33bl & br, 34bl, 35tl & tr, 66r, 68t, 71, 72, 73r, 74, 75l, 76, 77r.)

Sue Pearson, 13 Prince Albert Street, The Lanes, Brighton, East Sussex BN1 1HE, U.K, who can always offer the finest old bears. Sue allowed us to raid her shop one day and take her treasured bears away to be photographed in a nearby studio. (Bears on pages 11l, 12m, 13r, 17tr, 18, 20bm & br, 23bl, 26tr, 27bl & br, 30, 33t, 67br, 68b.)

Romy Roeder, who kindly provided us with photographs of some of her own Australian bears. (Bears on pages 29, 37r, 38, 39.)

Paul and Rosemary Volpp, who generously allowed us to use some specially selected examples from their superb Buck Hill Teddy Bear Collection. (Bears on pages 6r, 7br, 10, 11ltr & r, 12l & r, 13l, 14, 16, 27t, 31.)

All the artists who allowed us to illustrate this book with wonderful examples of their imaginative and creative teddy bears. Unfortunately it was not possible to include every bear that was photographed – our apologies to these bears and their owners. Thank you to the artists who lent their own bears. They appear on the following pages: 54br, 55m, 56tl, 61br, 57tm, 58tm, tr & br, 59tr & br, 60tl & tr, 61tl & tr, 62tl, tr & br, 63tl & 64tl & 65mr & bl, 70.

Bears on 53l courtesy of Margarete Steiff GmbH, 67bl courtesy of Anne Greaves and 54tl from a private collection. All other bears are owned by the authors and are either part of their private collection or can be found at their shop at 7 Cambridge Street, Wellingborough, Northants, NN8 1DJ, U.K.

Very special thanks to Quintet Publishing and the photographers, Nick Bailey and Jeremy Thomas, for all their patience.

And lastly a special thank you to daughter, Jenny, who managed to sort out our scribbles and type the manuscript.